THE CENTERING MOMENT

Also Available by Howard Thurman

The Centering Moment
The Creative Encounter
Deep is the Hunger
Deep River and the Negro Spiritual Speaks of Life and Death
Disciplines of the Spirit
Meditations of the Heart
Temptations of Jesus
The Growing Edge
The Inward Journey
Jesus and the Disinherited
Luminous Darkness
The Mood of Christmas
For the Inward Journey

Related Titles

Howard Thurman: Mystic as Prophet
A Strange Freedom

THE
CENTERING
MOMENT

BY HOWARD THURMAN

Friends
United Press
Richmond, Indiana • www.fum.org

Copyright 1969 by Howard Thurman
First Edition 1969 Harper & Row

Friends United Press, 101 Quaker Hill Drive, Richmond, IN 47374
First Edition 1980
Second printing 1984
Third printing 1990
Fourth printing 1991
Fifth printing 1994
Sixth printing 2000
Seventh printing 2007

Scripture quotation in prayer meditation Number 54 is from *The Bible, A New Translation* by James Moffatt, copyright 1954 by James A.R. Moffatt. Used by Permission of Harper & Row.

Scripture quotation in Numbers 32 and 79 from *The Holy Bible, Revised Standard Version*, copyright 1952 by Division of Christian Education of the National Council of Churches of Christ in the United States of America. Used by permission.

All other scripture quotations are from the Authorized Version.

Five-line quotation in Number 16 is from the hymn, "Dear Lord and Father of Mankind" by John Greenleaf Whittier.

Eight-line quotation in Number 86 is from "In Memoriam" by Alfred Tennyson.

Library of Congress Cataloging-in-Publication Data

Thurman, Howard, 1900-1981.
 The centering moment

 Reprint. Originally published: New York: Harper & Row, 1969.
 1. Meditations. 1. Title.
BV4832.2.2.T525 1984 242 80-67469
ISBN 978-0-913408-64-3

Dedication
In Memoriam
Edytha Macy Gross
Affectionately called "Babs"
Whose life "for-instanced"
Spontaneous Grace

Acknowledgments

Let my words of appreciation be given to the following persons whose labors and gifts made it possible for this book to be published:

Mrs. Alice Ratner, my secretary, who transcribed the basic texts from tapes and who typed the manuscript several times without boredom and without a loss of patience.

Mrs. Ellen Klemperer who pruned the first large section of material as it was taken from the tapes while preserving the essential quality of the spoken word.

Mrs. Anne Chiarenza, my daughter, who with professional skill checked and rechecked the total manuscript for unintentional repetitions, professional clichés, and other redundancies.

The many congregations who participated in these centering moments.

It is needless to add, but I do so, nevertheless, that the responsibility for the final form and content of these pages is mine and mine alone.

CONTENTS

The Prologue

This is a book of Prayer-Meditations winnowed out of a wide variety of meetings for worship. Some of them are topical in the sense that they reflect concern about contemporary events as they were happening in our immediate world. Others are windows into the brooding mind and quickened hearts of those who sensed the living God in their private struggles, needs, and predicaments. Although they were uttered by one voice functioning as the leader of worship, they carry an abiding sense of privacy and intimacy, as if that voice, and that alone, was sharing its innermost mood and thought with God. Some of them are stark and stripping —some of them reach into the vortex of social concern and focus on the ultimate responsibility of the individual before God.

They spring out of the tradition of Christian religious experience while they envelop needs and aspirations that are as universal as the human heart, as particular as human frailty, as intimate as the care of God for the fallen sparrow or as relentless as the ebb and flow of kingdoms and civilizations.

A rabbinical friend thinks of prayer as not a source but a result. "It is what a man does when he recognizes that he stands in the presence of God." He quotes Dr. Abraham Heschel as saying, "The issue of prayer is not prayer, the issue of prayer is God."

When a man prays he is not merely performing an act, he is *being* something. True it is that there are moving expressions which explode the anguish and the desires of the heart—there are moments when all that can be managed is the cry of pain or the unrestrained exultation of the spirit. Sometimes our utter fear is all that can be voiced, while underneath the words and manifestations is the sense of *being* in the presence of the Creator and Sustainer of life. The forms vary, the etiquettes are manifold, the traditions are diverse, the altars have meanings consecrated by generations of worshipers whose roots go back into a past without record and reckoning; but the *integrity* of prayer is ever constant— a man feels himself ultimately alone in the presence of God.

To Jesus, God breathed through all that is. The sparrow overcome by sudden death in its evening flight; the lily blossoming on the rocky hillside; the grass of the field and the garden path; the clouds light and burdenless or weighted down with unshed waters; the madman in chains or wandering among the barren rocks in the wastelands; the little baby in his mother's arms; the strutting arrogance of the Roman Legion; the brazen queries of the craven tax collector; the children at play or the old men quibbling in the market place; the august Sanhedrin fighting for its life amidst the impudences of Empire; the futile whisper of those who had forgotten Jerusalem; the fear-voiced utterance of the prophets who remembered—to Jesus God breathed through all that is. To him, God was Creator of life and the living substance; the Living Stream upon which all things moved; the Mind containing time, space, and all their multitudinous offsprings. And beyond all these God was Friend and Father.

The time most precious for him was at close of day. This was the time for the long breath, when all the fragments left by the commonplace, when all the little hurts and the big aches could be absorbed, and the mind could be freed of the immediate demand, when voices that had been quieted by the long day's work could once more be heard, when there could be the deep sharing of the innermost secrets and the laying bare of the heart and mind. Yes, the most precious time for him was at close of day.

But there were other times he treasured, "A great while before day," says the Book. The night had been long and wearisome because the day had been full of nibbling annoyances; the high resolve of some winged moment had frenzied, panicked, no longer sure, no longer free, then had vanished as if it had never been. There was the need, the utter urgency, for some fresh assurance, the healing touch of a healing wing. "A great while before day" he found his way to the quiet place in the hills. And prayed.

July, 1968　　　　　　　　　　　　　　HOWARD THURMAN
San Francisco

I

Ascriptions

*L*eave me not to the tempest of all the meaningful superficialities of my life, O God. Drive me, drive me, O God, to my inmost center where, stripped bare of all that cloys and clutters, I may know Thee even as I know me. This is the heart of the cry of Thy children, O God, holy God, our Father.

*A*ccept, our Father,
the offering of our faith
and our words and our lives.

*W*e seek forgiveness for the inadequacy
of mind and the slowness of heart
with which we seek to make
articulate the meaning of
Thy spirit within us,
O God, our Father.

*F*orgive us, O God, for all that is limiting and blind. Give the lift of Thy spirit to the desire of the heart as Thou dost know it.

In spite of feebleness of effort and great turmoil out of which here and there a light may come or a voice be heard, we thank Thee, O Father.

*F*orgive us, our Father,
for all the weaknesses
in our minds and spirits
and for all of the ways by which
the creative flow of Thy mind
and Thy spirit through us
may be frustrated and held at bay.

*F*orgive us, our Father, for all that remains standing between Thee and us: the fears and the anxieties, the hatreds, the bitternesses, the despair—forgive us for all these. Tutor our spirits in the hope that is born of Thy love for us, that we may learn in some way that speaks to our condition Thy love of Thee in us.

II

The Mood of Celebration

1. The Fragmentation of Our Days

Always our lives are surrounded by multitudinous witnesses of other moments, other days, other years. So much has entered into our living in other days that it is difficult to sort out the strands and locate the source. We gather together all of the fragmentation of our days. All the little things and the big things that have entered into our fulfillment up to this present moment. We take the long look, the very long look. We shudder as we become aware again of narrow escapes, of moments when we struck out against life (as creatures deep in pain) and, hurt and maimed, did violence to those we loved who trusted us and whom we trusted. We take the long look in the quietness. We are mindful of the gift of insight, of strength, of encouragement, of hope that turned up in our paths at a moment of our greatest despair and disillusionment, and our souls were lifted up and strengthened and our way confirmed—all of this as an act of grace without merit. This we see as we look back over the years.

We remember the resolutions, the high hopes. We recall the moments of distinct fulfillment when the heavens opened and all the world had a new smell. We look at the temptations that have won in our lives and at those over which we have been able to measure conquest and victory, when all the sons of God shouted for joy in our triumph. The times when we have been afraid and we have not known of what we were afraid. The times when we have wrestled with sickness and disease, and have managed somehow to tap resources of strength and healing, so that our bodies have rejoiced that it is well with us.

All of these things, and many more, crowd in upon us, our Father, as we offer to Thee the living substance of our days. No particular act of adoration of praise, but a total offering of all that we are we make to Thee, that Thou mayest take the long look, and bless and heal and redeem and sanctify. We want to feel Thy Presence and to have our minds renewed by Thy mind. Leave us not alone in our desiring, God, our Father.

2. *The Sacrament of Life*

We celebrate the sacrament of life, the simple delights of being alive with varying measures of health, strength, and vitality. We are blessed with so many things that we did not create ourselves, but are ours because of the labor, the work, the sacrifice, and the dreaming of many people whose names we shall never know— all of the little things by which our days are surrounded to make us secure, to make us happy, and to give to us a quiet sense of joy in being alive.

We make a sacrament of thanksgiving for all of these things, even as we remember those who are not blessed as we are blessed —the little children who are not comfortably housed, who do not have warm clothes to wear, who did not have breakfast this morning because there was no food for them; all of the frightened and lonely and desperate little children, all over the world—we remember them, in our comfort, in our plenty. In the quietness we seek to know how we may learn to be more sensitive, to be more charitable, to be more gracious, to be more sharing, if indeed we are to be true to ourselves. We make a sacrament of our determination to be better tomorrow than we are today, to be more thoughtful of our own needs and the needs of others, to be more gracious in the way we live, to the end that through us there shall come no violence to anyone; through no word of ours shall there be a heart broken, or a spirit injured. We make a sacrament of our determination in this regard, that we may be blessed by Thy spirit, O God, not because we are worthy or unworthy, but because we cannot live without Thy grace and benediction.

3. The Spirit of God Without—Within

How good it is to celebrate the spirit of God within us by quiet acts of adoration and praise; to remind ourselves of all of the ways by which His grace has watered the roots of our being, giving to us manifold strengths, creating miracle after miracle in the midst of the common task and the common way that we take; to respond to the movement of His spirit in our minds, guiding us into paths of truth where we labor under the necessity to think straight and carefully, to understand the integrity of the deeds which we perform. It is very good to celebrate the presence of the spirit of God in our lives by manifold acts of adoration and praise and quiet thanksgiving.

We share in the quietness and wide variety of common concerns. Though our personal needs are tailored to the measurements of our private lives, these needs, which are so intimately our own, mingle and become one with the needs of all who gather together in this moment. The overarching demands of the agonies of our times do not leave us untouched—the miseries of the children of men as they struggle in various parts of the world for fulfillment and for self-realization, all of those who are cut off from the normal intercourse of their lives by withering illness, and by despair and anguish which somehow cannot be shared—we are not unmindful of the agonies of our time as the movement of the spirit of God makes itself articulate in us.

We offer to Thee, our Father, our lives.
All of them.

4. Thanksgiving for Freedom

We make of our silence a paean of thanksgiving for Freedom. We make an offering of quiet gratitude to God for those men and women who in the darkness of an age lighted candles, first in their hearts, then in their families, then in the common way, that darkness might not triumph over the spirit of men.

We remember the light-bearers of life. We remember the moments in our own darkness when the way was lost and we became the sharers of the light brought into our darkness by a neighbor, the printed page, a kindly word gently spoken, a note written in tenderness and love.

We thank Thee that we have not been deserted by the Light.

The testimony of the Light reminds us that we are Thy children and that we need have no fear of the darkness—the darkness hideth not from Thee. The darkness and the light are both alike to Thee.

With great rejoicing we spread our thanksgiving before Thee.

5. Plotinus

The world, the cosmos, my little life, are contained in God, and if I keep the roadway open, even as I live, doing my thing in the world of things, I can keep journeying back home to be recentered, renewed, recreated, redeemed, over and over and over again, as long as I live and beyond.

For the assurance, our Father, of the movement of Thy spirit in the heart and mind and life of one whose language and whose culture and whose faith differed in so many crucial ways from our own but whose truth belongs to us, even as it belongs to Thee, we give uncluttered praise and thanksgiving. Walk beside us and in us, surrounding us with Thy love, that the way that we take may bring us safely to Thee, who is the source of all there is, the delight of our spirits, the God of our salvation.

6. The Day of Atonement

We join our brothers of the House of Israel as they assess, even as we ourselves do likewise, the stewardship of the common life, the private undertaking, and the individual enterprise. We are aware of the vast responsibility which is ours for the common life. In so many ways we have been silent when we should have spoken out. We have withheld the hand when we should have extended it in grace and in companionship. We have been blind to so much because we would not see. There are doors of truth into which we have not entered because of our preoccupation with lesser things and minor goals. In our private lives we have failed to meet the inner demands of our own conscience. We have done violence to the truth that is within us.

On the other side, there have been so many moments of wholeness in which we have participated, when we have felt purified, cleansed, and somehow redeemed. We have been surrounded by so much of grace and goodness in which we have shared consciously and deliberately. We have been cognizant of needs that extend beyond our household and our friends.

We acknowledge, then, before Thee, O God, our Father, the mixture of Life which is ours—so much that is unworthy, so much that is good. So many times, our Father, we have mounted upon wings as eagles because of the upward sweep of Thy spirit within us. So often we have groveled in the mud, unworthy of the good that we see.

We spread our lives out before Thee, complete and utter, seeking only that Thou wilt scrutinize them with the great wisdom that Thou hast accumulated. Pour out upon us in abiding measure Thy spirit, O living God, without which we stumble in the darkness and perish.

We are surrounded by so much grace + Goodness .

24

7. Christmas

This is the season of the year when so many things stand out in stark outline against the background of our days. We think of little children all over the world; children in refugee camps who have known aught else throughout the length of their days; children in orphanages in our own land and in other lands; rootless children who have no peg upon which to hang the identity of their meaning, but whose tender lives are cut adrift from all harbors of refuge and security; children in families where there is so little love that they are unaware that their own lives are touched by its gentleness and strength; sick children, those who have walked and will never walk again, those who have looked out on the beauty of the world and will never see it again. Our hearts are touched and melt in the quietness as we remember the children of the world.

We remember the old people. Those whose fires have been banked, and who sit in their solitariness, some with minds broken by the hardness of their days, who cannot be comforted by the memories of other times; some who at this season of the year hunger and thirst for the love of their children, and find it not; some who live in homes for the aged, surrounded by those of their kind, who huddle together, hoping that in the warmth of each other's personality and spirit they might find strength sufficient for another day.

God of our hearts and our lives, accept the tenderness which we pour out in our thoughts and in our memories and desires, and grant that it will inform our deeds, so that during these days that are upon us, to the limit of our strength and beyond, we may be messengers of Thy tidings, and sharers of Thy peace.

8. A New Year

The climate of silence gives clear meaning to the long shadows cast by the events of the year so recently passed: The high resolves with which we began it; the stumbling, faltering ways by which we ended it . . . The narrow escapes from violence, within, without . . . The high moments which in themselves seemed to contain all the goodness, beauty, and completeness of life . . . Those hours of sadness and weeping when there was taken from our midst someone whose life was deeply entwined with our own— since the leave-taking the way has been hard, difficult, with no bond to heal the ruptured life, the broken heart . . .

We do not quite know *how* to face the New Year, but face it we must. We do not know, our Father, nor do we wish to know what there is in store for us tomorrow. As we share the intimacy of this moment, quiet our spirits with Thy great calm that we may not be afraid, that we may be sustained whatever betides. This is not our only option, our Father, but we seize upon it, as if it were—we do it with enthusiasm and with hope. Desert us not to the despairing grasp of what may be our futilities, God of our spirits.

9. To Rest in His Presence

It is very good to turn aside from the rush and the weariness and the anxieties by which these days beset and lay seige to our moments, to rest in the presence of God. It is good to pause to make an end of so much that bothers and harasses the spirit, to assess the meaning of our lives in the light of the movement of the Spirit within us. These have been long months. For some they have been months of great taxation of spirit and pain of body and ache of heart. For some there was a time in the days that have passed beyond the sweep of our immediate experiencing when they felt that this day would never dawn for them. There are some for whom the past months have been freighted with anticipations, with hopes and dreams which were fulfilled and realized; and there are some for whom the hopes and dreams which kept alive the enthusiasms of their spirits were not realized and did not come to pass. We are surrounded by our own memories, and we are surrounded by the invisible cloud of witnesses to all of the stark and desolate moments of our race, framed by the vast uncertainties that surround each of our waking hours. Something of the contagion of these witnesses has entered into our own spirits, and we come to this place of pause and rest, scarcely able to realize that it is a moment of pause and a time of rest and renewal. We remember those persons known to us who will have no good tidings during this season, for whom there will be no star in the sky and whose ears will not hear the grand music of angelic hosts.

We search our hearts, our Father, as we wait here to see if it is within the depth and the height of our power and our strength to create in their desolate heavens not only a star by which their feet may be guided, but music that will quiet their fears and bring comfort to their spirits. Enable us, O God, even with our small and meager strength, so to be intent upon the sharing of that part of Thy spirit which is within us that for all and sundry, to a limit beyond our own strength, there may be a lift, a kindliness, a tenderness, a love which we share. We don't know how to do this exactly. We don't know. We do not even know, our Father, whether we have the right to seek Thy help. We only know that what Thou dost mean to us when we are most ourselves, by way of inspiration and joy and courage and hope, we so much would have Thee mean to all mankind everywhere. If we can help to do this, it will make our little joy complete. O God, God of our spirits, it will make our little joy complete.

10. To Celebrate His Goodness

It is very good to celebrate the goodness of God—the obvious expressions of this goodness that sustain our lives in ways that our strength could not quite do, in ways that our minds and even our imaginations cannot quite either comprehend or assess.

It is very good to celebrate the goodness of God for those miraculous manifestations of an intent, which is more than anything we can quite understand, and through which, when we have given up hope, hope refuses to die. The times when, having exhausted all of our own efforts, the insights we have been unable to find are suddenly ours; the wonderful sense that sins are forgiven, when we know there is within the grasp of our understanding no merit that is worthy of so great a boon; the sense of relief when a burden has been lifted or the guilt that bore us down, hounded us, has lost our scent, letting us escape from its necessities.

It is very good to celebrate the goodness of God even at times when we are apt to be overcome by our own sense of evil, even when we are most overcome by the oppressive mismanagement of the organized life around us.

"... hope refuses to die."

Hope (Christ)
is
Eternal.

29

11. *Jesus of Nazareth* I*

O sabbath rest by Galilee!
O calm of hills above,
Where Jesus knelt to share with Thee
The silence of eternity,
Interpreted by love!

In so many ways, ways beyond our own calculation and reflection, our lives have been deeply touched and influenced by the life and character, teaching and spirit, of Jesus of Nazareth. He moves in and out on the horizon of our days like some fleeting ghost. At times when we are least aware and often least prepared, some startling clear thrust of his mind moves in upon us, upsetting the normal tempo of our ways, reminding us of what we are, and what life is, giving to us sometimes judgment, sometimes a wistful murmur of the possibilities that lie before us, stirring within us resolutions, activating ancient desires, kindling anew dead hopes, giving to leaden spirits wings that sweep. We owe so much to the spirit which he let loose in the world. We think about it now in our meditation, gathering up all the fragments of our lives to see if for us there can be some creative synthesis, some wholeness, some great healing that will still our tempests and give to us the quiet trust that God is our Father, and we are His children living under the shadow of His spirit.

Accept our lives, O God; we ourselves do not know what to do with them. We place them before Thee as they are, with no suggestions, no hints, no attempts to order the working of Thy spirit upon us. Accept our lives, our Father.

* *The prayer-meditations I and II were spontaneous utterances of paragraphs written at an earlier time, and published in* The Inward Journey.

*Reminding us
of whose we are —
to whom we belong,
and where we're headed.*

12. *Jesus of Nazareth* II

We remember him whose life has so altered the life of the world. We relate to him, each one of us, after the pattern of our own upbringing, as well as in accordance with the most searching hunger of our own spirits. We find our lives strangely touched by his life when we give of ourselves to meet the needs of those about us: the cup of cool water to the thirsty; the tightening of the grip on a hand when the look in the eye reveals some pain beyond the reach of words; the reassurance to those who are sick when between you and them there is the unexpressed awarness that the sickness is unto death; the telephone call because the impulse to make it was so clear and strong; the simple desire to be better today than one was yesterday. Our lives are full of remembrances of his life which transcend the confession of our faith and the expression of the content of our religious devotion. And so we gather together, each one with his private way of remembering.

Thus, our Father, in these mute ways we give to Thee the praise of our hearts for the release into our world of one who did so much to make the burden of life more manageable and the carking cares that eat away at our peace less damaging. We are so very grateful to Thee, our Father, so very, very grateful.

The cup of cool water to the thirsty bro 7/or sister could take the form of Kindness, Gentleness 7/or Spiritual friendship.

31

13. The Watering of Our Roots

Surrounded by all of the memories and the dream and the hopes and the desires of so great a host of witnesses, we still ourselves in the presence of God, gathering together all of the things that are needful for our peace. The mood of thanksgiving overwhelms us when we remember how good and great is our fortune, even as we are mindful of the ways that are hard and difficult for so many whose names are known to us and whose pictures are vividly in our minds. It is so great a privilege to experience the watering of one's roots at a time of such dryness in the world.

Thus, our Father, we expose ourselves to Thy spirit, daring not at all to make even the simplest request of Thee. We let ourselves down in Thy grace and Thy holiness, waiting for the movement of Thy spirit.

III

No Man Is
an Island

14. *Right Relations with Others*

Always we live under some necessity for righting our relations with our fellows. We turn to the scrutiny of the light in our hearts to see wherein we have lived without harmony, without order, and without an increasing measure of tranquillity and peace. We look at the misunderstandings which we have experienced during the week that has passed. Those moments when our words conveyed what was not our intent, and the result of their movement into the life of another, brought chaos and pain and misery. Those moments when with clear-eyed intent we have gone out of our path to do the vengeful thing, to speak or to act with hardness of heart. We remember all of our reactions to the ill will in the world, to the bitterness that has loomed large between peoples and states, between countries, and between nations. All of these things weigh heavily upon our minds and spirits as we seek somehow within ourselves to be whole and clean and purified.

Our Father, we come to Thee, seeking in quiet ways the courage to ease the tensions and break the discord in which, in one way or another, our lives are sourrounded. We offer to Thee the treasures of our life, to the end that we may be so touched by Thy spirit and sensitized by Thy love and Thy tenderness that we may find our way in peace and in strength and in confidence. This is what we seek, even as we worship Thee, O God, in spirit and in truth.

15. Ties of Blood

We remember those who are close to us by ties of blood and accommodation, whose needs have been exposed to us in the days that are behind; those who are sick and who are moving slowly into a terminal dimension of their illness; those who have fallen upon hard and difficult times, from whose hands have been snatched those symbols of security by which the tranquillity of their lives has been measured; those who are dependent upon us for things which we cannot give and we do not know how to say that we cannot give them. We remember those men and those women whose private lives are burdened by the responsibilities of others and who find, because of the problems which surround them, that their private lives are inadequate and they are lonely and frightened and dismayed. We remember all who stand within the shadow of the radiance that belongs to the healthy mind and the vigorous spirit; those who are wrestling with inner tortures that pull the world out of balance, who find themselves retreating more deeply within in the hope that in the iron-bound security of their inmost privacy they may be protected from the things that overwhelm and prove unmanageable.

We remember ourselves, all our needs, our joys, our sorrows, our hopes, our anxieties, our fumblings for the light, our sins, our violences; we remember ourselves, our Father. Accept us as we are, without any of the pretensions by which we live from day to day, but as we are, within our predicament and our life; and, if we may be assured in the quietness that underneath us is Thy sustaining strength, then we shall have no fear of tomorrow, and no anxiety about the road which stretches before us.

"Let the words of my mouth, and the mediation of my heart, be acceptable in thy sight, O Lord, my strength, and my redeemer."

16. The Totality of Our Lives

We bring to this moment of sacrament the totality of our lives. There is a sense in which each of us is sealed off from the other, a sense in which each of us wrestles with his own needs, desires, frustrations, limitations, aspirations, joys, sorrows, sickness, and health. There is another sense in which we are deeply involved in the common life, the common struggle, common needs, desires, the common burdens. We blend all that we are as individuals, and wait in the quietness for the movement of the Spirit and the Mind of the living God in our midst. *Beautiful*

We rejoice, our Father, that it is given unto us to sense Thy presence, to know our own needs as seen by the light of Thy countenance, and we give to Thee our thanks for all of the promises of renewal, of healing, of redemption, that we have experienced from the days of our birth; for all of the light that has been cast on our pathway in moments of great darkness; for the strength that came when all that we could understand and know was weakness; for the sense that we are not alone. We thank Thee, O God, our Father, for this assurance. We offer as earnest of our thanksgiving the quiet resolution of our hearts to be true, tomorrow and tomorrow, more fully than we have ever been before, to Thy spirit within us, that in what we do and say and think and experience, we may give joy to Thy heart and peace to our spirits. Without this we perish as children of the night. God, our Father, teach us how to be Thy children.

17 Our Minor Absolutes

It is very hard for us to be in Thy presence. There are so many minor absolutes to which we give our strength and our energies that we are embarrassed before Thee. Wilt Thou give, out of the great stretches and detachment and calm that give birth to the dreams that Thou hast poured so lavishly upon us, some insight that will tutor us in quiet, in silence, and in waiting? We seek forgiveness, but again and again as we wait in the silence, we do not quite know for what. Perhaps what we really seek is an awareness of sin and failure, shortcomings. Thus we spread these out before Thee. Thou knowest. We would be better than we are, but as we wait in Thy presence we are not sure that we want to be better than we are. There is so much reassurance in the comfort of our life; so much confidence has been built up in us in the familiar role and the familiar style of our life. If under the aegis of Thy spirit our lives were changed, we are afraid, our Father, of what might become of us. Work over us, knead us, do to us what our spirits require, not that we may be better than we are, our Father, but that we may more deeply *desire* to be better than we are.

We would not spend all of our time in this waiting silence pre-occupied with our own needs and our own little lives. We would be mindful of those others to whom we are related by recollection and by devotion. We would remember those whose lives move in areas of which we are not aware and with which we are not familiar, whose names and whose language we do not speak or understand—the great, vast desolation of Thy children. We would remember this even as we savor the essence of our own comfort and security. We would remember those men who stand at the strategic spots of power in the world, making decisions as if they were gods and on whose decisions so much of the destiny of Thy children depends. O God of human spirits, leave them not to the strength of their weaknesses or the weakness of their strengths, but brood over them, nudging them, urging them, tutoring them with Thy love and Thy patience, until at last they may find a way to seek Thy wisdom.

Drop Thy still dews of quietness,
Till all our strivings cease;
Take from our souls the strain and stress,
And let our ordered lives confess
The beauty of Thy peace.

O God, our Father.

18. The Little Graces of Life

Our Father, we turn aside from the things that ordinarily occupy our waking hours and we wait in Thy presence. We are reminded of the graces of life that are so commonplace, so much a part of our daily living that the grace of them is lost sight of. Each day for many days we have been able to arise from our beds and be active, to do our work, to live our lives with the full function of our bodies. Each day we have been greeted by a few people who understand us and who salute us. We have been smiled upon, we have been blessed by the countenances of many of Thy children. The little graces of life.

We have been visited also, our Father, by concerns to which we have responded, sometimes with enthusiasm and conviction; and other times we have been so overwhelmed with our own personal needs and disorders and complexities that we have not had any time to give to the needs and disorders and complexities of other people, and we feel just a little guilty about it as we linger in the quietness, sorting out the details of our lives. We do not want to have hard hearts, we do not want to close the windows of our spirits to the cries and to the agonies of those whose needs cry out to Thee. There seems to be no ear to hear, no hand to succor. We do not wish to be this way, but our own lives are hard and our frustrations are very great. Thus, our Father, we try to loosen ourselves up, so that we may become aware of what it is that Thou art seeking to do in us and in our world, so that after this hour we may not only be refreshed and renewed but we may be on the scent of that which is Thy will for us. To know Thy will, O God, and to sink these little minds and little purposes of ours into Thy will—this is the heart of our hunger, O God of our spirits, as we wait in Thy presence.

19. For the Students of the World

We pray for the students of the world:

Those in refugee camps who are straitened by the vast uncertainties of all their waking moments.

Those in Egypt, Israel, South Africa, Europe, and all the centers of the earth where they live and learn.

Those in our own land who are lonely, homeless, aimless, confused, dedicated.

We pray for the students of the world!

We hold ourselves and them steadily, quietly, with great concentration before Thy altar. Invade their lives, their living contexts, their surroundings, not only with Thy wisdom and understanding but also with Thy judgment and its vitality, to the end that something will become manifest in them that will make Thy kingdom, Thy rule, effective in the way that they take. We do not ask. We do not plead. We do not beg. We offer them and ourselves and we wait. In Thy presence we wait; Thou wilt not reject our spirits.

20. The Moment of Recollection

In Thy presence, our Father, we make an act of recollection:

We cradle in tenderness those that have been visited by sudden or muted violences; families shattered by death and murder; those distraught by illness which does not respond to the trained mind and the skilled hand; those who inhabit the shadows where things are never clear to the mind and at the core of whose spirit lies an endless torture, making for restlessness, panic, and madness; children who are without love and compassion, who must manage life with ill-formed and blunted tools; the lonely who cannot experience the penetration of the wall that envelops them; and those who are so tired that the ground of their being is consumed by a great weariness. These we remember before Thee, our Father.

We do not know how to express our feelings, we do not know quite what to say. We give to Thee a cloud of witnesses to human need that in Thee may be found sanctuary for them. As for us, we still ourselves in Thy presence to be caught up by the movement of Thy spirit in our minds and hearts so that we may dare become Thy living agents of usefulness and redemption. Grant, O gracious God, that we may not betray Thy urgency through self-love, self-pity, or fear. This our souls cannot abide. Deliver us from so great a temptation, our Father.

21. Mindful of the Agonies

We are mindful of the agonies that are sweeping over our world. Suffering, hunger, disaster falling upon whole communities and generations; fears that drive nations to put their organized might against other nations' organized weakness; the utter loneliness of those whose dwelling place is the solitude of vast havoc; the anguish of sensitive spirits that find no windbreak against the impact of so much human misery. From all this there is no escape. As if this were not enough. We are immobilized by our private world of frustration and inner chaos, of needs unfulfilled, of dreams that leave us bereft of even the hope of fulfillment.

Surround us, close present God of our spirit, that we may fathom the true intent of our hearts and our strivings, that we may sense the true intent of Thy purpose in human history, and the personal enterprise. We would not turn away from Thee; but again and again it is so hard to find Thee. Find Thee we must. Understand us in our searching, that even our weakness may lead us to Thy dwelling place.

22. Far-flung Needs of Thy Children

Our Father, we would bring Thee, as we offer our prayer, the far-flung needs of Thy children everywhere. Some needs we recognize as part and parcel of the full or limited measure of our own responsibilities. Some needs seem far removed from where we are, they but underscore the littleness and impotence of our own lives. We would share all of this with Thee, our Father, but our minds and our hearts are caught and held by our own private predicaments and our own great personal needs. So wilt Thou understand us and deal gently with us, as out of the private life with which we are so utterly familiar we speak to Thee about the concerns of our hearts?

We are mindful that we are sinners, and when we say this, our Father, we are not thinking of ways by which we have not conformed to some great external law or doctrine or theology. When we say, our Father, that we are sinners, we are talking very personally to Thee about our own experiences, of our own limitations —all the mean things to which, either in moments of weakness or of pride, we have yielded. The bad thoughts that we have had even as our faces were smiling and our eyes were glowing . . . The things that we have refrained from doing, when we felt the urge to do them because they were right and decent and whole and clean . . . This is what we mean, our Father, as we talk to Thee about our sins. Wilt Thou forgive us, that we may try again to make it where we have failed before?

Our fears, our Father, are very present. We know that there is no occasion in all the quietness to talk of the tempest and the tortures of our private fears. But they are a part of our lives: the fear of sickness and bodily failure, fear of desertion and loneliness, fear for our jobs, fear of the instability of our own economic lives, fear for our families and our children, fear of life itself. It is so wonderful, our Father, as we talk with Thee about this, that the fears are not always present, that there are moments when we are free and our very spirits take wing, and all the things that imprison and hold are left behind, and we look down upon them from afar

44

and wonder why they could hold such sway over our lives. These moments come to us and we thank Thee for them. May we remember them when the fears close in upon us.

Our dreams are before us and before Thee, the dreams which we had forgotten until, in the quietness, all the stillness before Thee brings them back with their living touch. The plans we had made for our lives at some earlier time, and the way we had hoped that the future would unfold before us. Somewhere along the way something happened to us, the dream faded, somehow we took a wrong turn in the road—we don't know. But fingering the dreams of our lives, our hearts yearn for a fulfillment which has never been ours.

O God, keeper of the dreams of Thy children, leave us not alone, leave us not alone. Be in us and about us even as Thy spirit does surround us, to the end that we may take courage, without which, our Father, our very spirits sicken and die. O God, who will not let us go, teach us how to hold fast to Thee.

23. The Common Mood

It is a very blessed thing to be privileged to share together the common mood, the full and searching moment in which the meaning of the private life is lifted up and seen in a perspective as broad as life and as profound. Again and again we are overwhelmed by the littleness of our lives, the way in which there seems to close in upon us the intimate need, the personal demand. There is often no breathing moment that permits us to lift up our heads and take the long look and sense ultimate meanings in which our lives are involved. Thus each has his world of need and necessity and urgency; some of us are wrestling with very great anxieties. We do not know how to deal with that which awaits us tomorrow, and in our desperation and our panic we find ourselves unable to center our spirits upon the meaning of this great and significant moment in our lives. There are some who are ill and we have no way by which we can determine now what this illness says about the length of our lives. We wrestle with this secondary undertone of uneasiness while we await the revelation of the trained mind and the skilled hand. There are some who are deeply troubled about the state of the world—the fever that seems to be sending our civilization hurtling along a path which threatens to end in destruction and carnage and great tragic waste. So we clutch this moment of intimacy and friendliness and put it over against all the darkness that seems to be brooding over the nations of the world. There are some who remember the meaning of this day in the richness and tradition of the faith, and we seek ways by which we may enter into its meaning in our own way so that there will be in us no thing that will spoil the fullness of the joy of the moment of triumph.

Here we are, our Father, all of us Thy children, each with his own life and world and need. We lay gently upon Thy altar our life as it is, and we hold it there, waiting for Thy Spirit to invade our spirits so that we shall be prepared for the living of our lives, whatever may be the circumstances by which our days, tomorrow and tomorrow, may be surrounded. For this, O God, we utter in the quietness our thanks and our praise.

24. *The Mob in Mississippi*

Once again all men of tender heart are disturbed because of the evil tidings of the violence of the mob that moves in Mississippi. We feel in our own bodies the panic and the fear and the pain and the agony of the victim. We feel in our own minds and spirits the violence and the hate and the fear and the insecurity and the discomfort of those who have made of another human being a victim. We settle ourselves in the midst of our own guilt and uneasiness of mind and spirit. We sense our shame, our humility, and in some measure our helplessness. Great and profound are the questions that turn over in our minds as we contemplate the meaning of the deed.

O God, who must somehow understand what Thou seest in us, we have no words with which we come before Thee. The long string of our contrition and our alibis disintegrates in our hand. We would seek Thy forgiveness but we do not quite know how, our Father. We offer our predicament to Thy scrutiny and Thy love, with the great and agonizing hope that our experience may not confound Thy wisdom and our frustration may not put Thee to rout. We wait for the consolation that only Thou canst give, O God, our Father.

25. We Want To Be Understood

Again and again we are baffled by the confusion which we experience when we try to make clear to another what it is that our hearts would say and our minds would think. We want to be understood, to be sure that the word will be tenderly held and that the mood which is our mood will be deeply and profoundly shared. Again and again this is not our experience. We turn our eyes sometimes outward, casting a spell of judgment upon the words of others, the deeds of others, the moods of others. Sometimes when we are most ourselves, the eye turns inward and we are surprised to discover that what we did share was what we intended to share, that the searching honesty of our own hearts is something with which we ourselves are not acquainted. This is our experience with ourselves and with each other.

Waiting in the presence of God, we seek gingerly to find a way by which we may be honest—honest in our thoughts *now*, honest in our feelings *now*, honest in our desirings *now*.

"For there is not a word in my tongue, but, lo, O Lord, thou knowest it altogether. Thou hast beset me behind and before, and laid thine hand upon me. Search me, O God, and know my heart; try me, and know my thoughts; And see if there be any wicked way in me, and lead me in the way everlasting."

26. Reaping and Sowing

The long arm of the relentless logic of reaping and sowing gathers within the sweep of its judgment the innocent and the guilty, the responsible and the irresponsible, the weak and the strong, the old and the young. The heavy shadow of the threat of war is upon us, and as we search our own hearts we find we are at war within ourselves. We recognize the failure of the things upon which we have pinned our hopes. We recognize the hopes that have not deserted us, even in these strange times loaded with stranger events, and we long for some authentic word that will speak peace to our hearts and peace to the nations of the earth. Even as we long for this, our guilt looms ever before us. We are wanderers with shattered spirits, offering in the quietness our fragments.

Our Father, we do not know how to pray to Thee. We do not know what we have the right to say to Thee. We do not even know how we feel. All that we know is that our peace is choked by the threat that lingers menacingly over all our waking hours, making our sleep fretful and unrewarding. Give unto us guidance. Give unto those in whose hands rests the immediate decision—guidance. Tame the stupidity and the greed and the avarice and the fear out of the souls of the peoples of this earth, that Thy purposes for Thy children may not be thwarted and frustrated because of the blindness in our thoughts and the fear in our hearts. Our Father, Creator of life, Sustainer of the generations of men, leave us not alone, leave us not alone.

27. The Tight Circle

Each one of us is mindful of the tight circle in which his life is lived. Aware of the other presences by which we are surrounded, each has his private world of thoughts and aspirations and needs. We remember those within the sweep of our concern and affection who are ill, some with diseases that are terminal in character. We watch these loved ones as for them, day by day, there is the experience of the closing of the doors. We remember those whose minds are eclipsed and who spend their hours moving in the shadows where nothing quite seems to declare itself. We watch them as their minds tremble in a crazed place, and our hearts break with the desire for their healing and their restoration. We remember the little children who have no recollection of mother or father, whose days are spent in the grim struggle for life and survival, whose little nervous systems are distorted and twisted and misshapen, whose little minds and spirits seem to have no chance to blossom and unfold. We remember those in whose hands rest the decisions that can determine peace or war for our time. We remember ourselves, each one of us in his tight little place, the anxieties, the sins, the sorrows, the joys, the hopes, the fears. All of these and more than mind can grasp and heart can feel crowd in upon us.

Our Father, as we settle ourselves in Thy presence, brood over our lives with the long-time wisdom which Thou hast distilled from Thy experiences with life and dreams, to the end that there may come into our lives some fleeting glimpse of purpose and meaning and redemption, that we may be purged and cleansed, renewed and strengthened, to the end that we may be willing to do Thy will and to walk in Thy way. For us, O God, our Father, this is enough.

28. Our Hearts Are Wooed

Again and again we find ourselves deeply distressed because there is so much that is dependent upon us as individuals carrying specific responsibilities within a world which is small and compact and demanding. So overwhelming is this kind of pressure upon us that we are tempted to rely, despite all of our inadequacies, upon our own strength. Again and again we say to ourselves, if I do not depend upon myself, if I do not depend upon that which I am able to do for myself and those for whom I am responsible, then there is no other source upon which I may be dependent. And even as we say it and as we feel it, our minds are flooded with multitudinous instances in which strength did come to us that was not of our making, a lift to our burden did come, even though it could not be measured by anything that we ourselves were doing. All around us there are these surprises of kindly interference manifesting the grace of life and the tenderness and the mercy of God.

Thus our hearts are wooed into thanksgiving and praise for so much that has come to us, transcending our merit and our demerit, so much thoughtfulness, so much reassurance, so many little ways by which our spirits have been renewed and revived. Even against our disposition, we offer our thanksgiving to Thee. Accept it, our Father, as our sacrament and as our offering to Thee, totally, wholeheartedly, that after this hour has passed each may know for himself that he is Thy child and Thou art his Father.

Our times are in Thy hand.

29. *Forgive Us Our Blindness* I

There are errors of the mind which make for the bad judgment when things seem to be distorted, twisted, and misshapen: an innocent remark comes from us as the word that hurts, shocks, or makes afraid, turning a friend into an enemy; a decision is made in utter haste before there is time for the wisdom of one's years to yield assent; a need is turned away from our door because we are sure that it is not what it seems—it is so easy to be "taken in," or so it seems.

Forgive us our blindness.

There are moments of authentic callousness or hardness of heart when we are not aware of the barb in the spoken word or the shattering sequence in the life of another following from the reckless act that ignores, passes over, or degrades. There are other times when we rise to the defense of our own pride of position and place, thus rendering deep insecurity to someone who looked to us for the encouraging word and the compassionate glance, when we responded without mind to the urgent request which sprang full grown out of another's pain . . .

Forgive us our blindness.

Father, grant us the awareness that opens wide the doors of our hearts, that will make us in our way keep a sense of what is vital in others, even as our lives become more and more transparent and of no harm to anyone.

30. Forgive Us Our Blindness

The goodness of our fortune is etched against the background of many tidings of great suffering in our land, the thousands of families that have found it necessary to seek shelter in places of refuge not their own, the many filled with the desperation known only to those who stand helplessly in the presence of suffering and anguish and need which they cannot meet. Against the background of the hunger of the world is the fullness of our stomachs. Against the background of the sickness of the world is our private experience of health. We would remember the needy. This is so difficult to do, so very difficult.

Grant, our Father, that the persistent pressure of Thy needy children will tenderize our spirits and make soft our hearts, that each of us in his own way will find a means to give expression to the impulse inspired by the movement of Thy spirit within us. This is how we want to feel, this is how we want to behave, our Father. Forgive us for our blindness; forgive us for our hardness of heart; forgive us for the arrogance of our comfort. Forgive us, O God, and grant that we may be so touched at the quiet place in our hearts and lives, that we may even dare to give ourselves, to give ourselves.

31. We Are Visited

It is our great and blessed fortune that our lives are never left to themselves alone. We are visited in ways that we can understand and in ways that are beyond our understanding, by highlights, great moments of inspiration, quiet reassurances of grace, simple manifestations of gratuitous expressions of the goodness of life. These quiet things enrich the common life and give to the ordinary experiences of our daily grind a significance and a strength that steady and inspire. We are also surrounded by the witness of those others whose strivings have made possible so much upon which we draw from the common reservoir of our heritage, those who have carried the light against the darkness, those who have persevered when to persevere seemed idiotic and suicidal, those who have forgotten themselves in the full and creative response to something that calls them beyond the furthest reaches of their dreams and their hopes.

We are surrounded also by the witness of the life of the spirit in peculiar ways that speak directly to our hearts and to our needs: those men and women who walk the pages of the holy book; those men and women with whom in our moments of depression and despair, and in our moments of joy and delight, we identify.

We are grateful to Thee, our Father, for all of the springs of joy and renewal and recreation that are our common heritage and our common lot. We offer in thanksgiving to Thee the fruits of our little lives,, that they may in turn be to others a source of strength and inspiration, that apart from us they may not find fulfillment and apart from them we may not know ourselves.

We thank Thee, our Father, for so holy a privilege and we offer our thanksgiving, our dedication, and our response, not only to Thee, but to the life which is ours.

32. The Healing of the Silent Breach

We are reminded in many ways of the quiet ministry of the spirit of the living God in our lives and in life that abounds around us. The little healings of the silent breaches, the great redemptive acts when times are out of joint, the lifting of our horizons of hope when to have hope seems to be against all wisdom and against all judgment, the stirring of the will to forgive when for so long a time we have been buried under an avalanche of great hostilities—there are so many ways by which the ministry of the living God tutors the spirit, corrects the times, gives lift to the days.

Today we are reminded of these graces, and we turn as best we may with all of our minds and hearts to Thee, O God, offering our thanksgiving, our gratitude, that Thou hast not left us alone. It is not because we are worthy or unworthy. It is not because we are good or bad, desperate or abounding in hope, but because we are Thy children and Thou art our Father. We don't know how to put into words the things that stir within us at such a time, but we wait in Thy presence, until at last Thou dost speak to Thyself through us, and even the travail of our souls is satisfied.

"Let the words of my mouth and the mediation of my heart be acceptable in thy sight, O Lord, my rock and my redeemer."

33. The Things That Weigh Heavily

Our minds are full of all of the involvements, issues, and problems of our daily living. The smell of the world is upon us. Sometimes it is very hard to tear ourselves away from the things that tax us and weigh heavily upon us, moment by moment, hour by hour, day unto day; and yet there is a quiet joy in us because we are privileged to withdraw, to turn aside. We gather in one bundle if we can, or as we can, the totality of our individual lives. We finger all of the meaning of our private experiences, our hopes, our ambitions, our fears, our joys, our sorrows. As we do this, we turn, each in his own way, to something more than we are, to a spirit, to an atmosphere, to a silence, to a presence; with the hope that what has been anxiety for us may be tranquilized by this presence, what has been low may be lifted and purified, redeemed and established; what has been weakness will be redone by the presence, until at last weakness becomes strength; what has been despair may become hope, what has been sickness may become health.

Our hearts overflow with thanksgiving, our Father, that such is our privilege, such is Thy tenderness and Thy mercy. We offer as our sacrament this sentiment of our hearts, this enthusiasm of our spirits, that Thou mayest be to us now that which pleases Thee most deeply; for to yield satisfaction to Thy spirit, O God, is the be-all and the end-all of our desires.

34. Overwhelming Gratitude

There is the sense of overwhelming gratitude which is ours because life has continued to unfold within us and about us, so that we have a full measure of strength and vigor; overwhelming gratitude for all the graces of renewal by which our lives are sustained, nestled, and nurtured; overwhelming gratitude that it is as well with us and our land as it is. There are also within us anxiety, contrition, and embarrassment because we have not been mindful of the needs of others even in accordance with the light that is within us. Aware of our fullness of stomach, our spirits are harassed and bewildered by the cries of the hungry. In the midst of so much that surrounds us with security, our minds and hearts are distressed because of the vast numbers of our brethren who live on the ragged edge of all meaning and for whom one more day of life is one more day of madness and torture.

And yet, our Father, we have no live option but to lay bare before Thee, as in one simple, tight panorama, the entire story of our lives, leaving out no thing, no private, hidden secrecy of the heart, no desire, however remotely removed from what we recognize as the conscious act and the conscious deed.

We spread before Thee in the quietness, our Father, our lives. We hold them there, waiting, waiting for the movement of Thy spirit upon the waters, waiting, our Father, waiting. Leave us not alone with our little selves, O God of our spirits, God of our lives.

35. The Hunger of the Hungry

It is good to have a long moment in which to sort out many things that stir within us, to look at our desires and to watch them take shape before our enchanted eyes while we measure the meaning of their fulfillment. To examine the network of relationships by which we are bound to others and by which others are bound to us, and to weight these relationships in the light of what seems to us in moments of transcendent clarity to be our true intent. To sense the private and collective guilt that stands always on the edges of our minds, casting its gloom and its shadow, sometimes dark and heavy, sometimes light and shifting, but always the shadow. To see the bearing of these shadows on the light that our own lives cast. To look at the dead places in ourselves, those things which we have watched die because there was no nourishment we were able to give, or because in our fear of life we strangled them to death. To look at the dead places in our lives and contemplate the awful vitality of a great resurrection. To feel the fear of the panic-stricken in our world, to feel the hunger of the hungry, the loneliness of the lonely, the sickness of the sick, and to wish with all our hearts that we might live our lives dedicated to ends more worthy than those by which we have lived up to this waiting moment.

All this we finger and feel quietly, solitarily, in the midst of Thy presence, O God! We have no words to offer Thee, no words by which we may bring Thy will into our ken. We wait for the stirring of Thy spirit in our hearts, and in this moment our hearts say "yes." And this is enough, our Father.

36. Creatures of Pain and Hurt

We are buffeted about by so rich a variety of circumstances that it is often very difficult for us to find our own ways. We are creatures of pain and hurt, of joy and ecstasy, of despair and hope. All around us we see great stretches of unrelieved human misery: hunger of body, with all the wasting away of the flesh that comes in its wake; upheaval of mind, with all of the inward torture with which the skill of man finds no way to deal. We are surrounded by so much that casts doubt and so often so little that uplifts and inspires. And when we think about our own selves, each within the tight circle of his little life, the same picture presents itself. We have found no satisfying answer for the pain of our lives.

At such a time as this, our Father, enveloped by the great quietness instilled by Thy presence, we want to offer the part of us that is clear, unsullied, fresh, clean, untainted, and to hold back under the shadow of our own feelings the things that are tainted and painful and tragic.

Teach us, our Father, how we may be so worthy of our living experience, that we may even now offer to Thee our pain, our suffering, our miseries—all the stains of our lives, even as we offer to Thee our best. What a relief it is, O God, to have somewhere to pour it all out. Our Father, our Father, accept us totally.

37. The Smell of Life

Each of us comes to Thee with his private world of meanings and desires. Each one of us has the smell of life upon him. There are concerns that lie heavily upon us this day—the great unsettled issues that are so fraught with fatal options that center in different spots of the world: in Formosa, in the Near East, in North Africa and South Africa, in Virginia, in Arkansas. Some of us have heaviness of heart as we identify with Martin King as he wrestles for his life in the Harlem Hospital, and we move gently into the tortured brain and fevered spirit of her whose anguish was so great that in the blindness of her own spirit she struck out as a thing in pain. We remember ourselves, the high hopes, the enthusiasms, the searching uneasinesses and anxieties with which we begin our new year. And we wait, O God our Father, in Thy presence, spreading before Thee in the simplest way our hearts can define and determine, our lives and our plans and our dreams.

Thou hast had long experience with Thy children through all the ages of their climb. Out of the wisdom which is Thine wilt Thou deal tenderly with what Thou seest in us, reminding us in all the ways that Thy creative mind can conjure, that if we nourish that which is a sickness we shall corrupt ourselves, that if we nourish within ourselves those things that are false, we shall pervert ourselves, that if we nourish those things that are out of the light, we shall spend our days stumbling through the darkness. Teach us, O God, God our Father, how we may so live that the richness of all the staggering possibilities of life may find its way into the path we take.

38. Tidings of Destruction

We spread before Thee, our Father, all of the mounting concerns of our lives and even as we do so we are not sure of what Thou canst do about them. But there is within us the great necessity to expose the heights and the depths of our concerns to Thee, whose wisdom transcends our little wisdoms, whose caring contains all the reaches of our own love, and whose mind holds all our little minds in their place.

We are concerned as we hear the tidings of the destruction and the suffering from the raging storms and the winds and the snows of winter, as in combination they beat down upon Thy children in other lands. The suffering, the desolation, the panic, the fear— these reach us even in the quietness. The concern that we feel for France and for that section of North Africa where so much violence and so much evil have been done. We try to encompass in the sweep of our awareness the intimate overtones of colossal misery and frustration and hurt and pain and hate and love. One by one we might speak of our various desires. But Thou knowest how far these reach and where they are limited and bounded by our ignorance or our indifference or by the intensity of the personal struggle with which we ourselves are faced.

We lay bare the personal concerns of our private lives: the decisions we must make and do not know how to make; the anxiety which we feel because of what is going on within our minds or our bodies, the outcome of which we cannot even guess. The little awareness of the little problems of our little lives mounts to overwhelming proportions when we still ourselves in Thy waiting presence. We ask nothing. We wait. We wait, our Father, until at last something of Thy strength becomes our strength, something of Thy heart becomes our heart, something of Thy forgiveness becomes our forgiveness. We wait, O God, we wait.

39. We Have Failed To Love

Our Father, we count ourselves privileged to think our deepest thoughts and feel our most authentic feelings in Thy presence. We are guilty of straying away from the truth as we have sensed it and felt it, at times, when the light within us was very clear. Sometimes we have done this because we were not aware of our straying. Sometimes we have done it because we chose to take a step merely because we wanted to do it and all questions of oughtness were set aside. We have failed to love where it was clear that to love was a necessity of the mind and of the heart. We have indulged ourselves in smallnesses, little hostilities, little meannesses, and now we are mindful of them in a strange and striking manner. Wilt Thou purge us of our sins? We do acknowledge them before Thee and plead no extenuating circumstances: we did as we did; we behaved as we behaved; and we seek cleansing and purification and renewal of our hearts and our minds.

We remember those people who are close to us by birth or by kinship or by sustained association or by other ties that bind us to them and them to us. Some of them are sick; some are distressed. Whatever may be their condition, our Father, we presume to share that condition with Thee even as we share that condition with ourselves. We would name them but this is not necessary. Thou knowest and we know and we remember.

We are concerned today, our Father, about many things, some of them superficial, some very important to us: our own well-being, our health, the dreams which we have but which have been shaken by circumstance, all of the little things that go to make up the meaning of our private lives. These things we recall one by one, or in great groups we lay them before Thee even as we lay ourselves before Thee. Whatever there is in us, our Father, that does not delight Thy heart; whatever there is in us that deepens Thy anxiety for Thy children; whatever there is in us that will prove to be defeating and destructive, from the long look that Thou hast before and behind, wilt Thou teach us how to purge it, how to redirect our lives, how to reorder our purposes so that the longer we live, the more we will come into creative and full possession of ourselves? This is a part of the stirring of our hearts and of the thoughts that focus themselves in our minds as we wait in the stillness for the movement of Thy spirit, Thy spirit upon us, and in us, and about us, O God, our Father.

40. Rekindle Our Memories

It is good to refresh our minds and rekindle our memories and remember the little graces by which our lives have been sustained: food to eat, water to drink, rest after labor, the renewal of energies which seem somehow to come automatically to our bodies and to our minds. There are so many graces by which our lives are sustained, and we remember them as we come before God. We remember the little acts of kindness that came our way from some unsuspected source, a smile at a moment when a smile could penetrate to the very deeps of our being, a warm handshake when we needed it most, a letter, a telephone call, a little package. We remember all of the simple gratuitous acts of kindness that have come to our lives from the lives of others. We remember all of these as we wait in the presence of God. We remember those whom we love and who love us. We remember those whom we would love but do not quite know how. We remember those we love and find it hard to trust. We remember those from whom have come to us the things that hurt, that wound, that bruise, that create anguish. We remember them as we wait in the presence of God. We remember our own world and those who make the great decisions that affect our lives: the President of the United States, the Secretary of State, the governors, the policemen on the beat, the firemen, those who collect the refuse and the garbage. We remember those whose decisions affect our common life, even though at point after point we are not involved in those decisions.

Thus, O God, our Father, we spread before Thee the entire panoply of our lives, the things that we affect and the things that affect us. And we seek to find a way to look at them, a way to feel about them, that is in accordance with Thy will and Thy purpose and Thy concern. We do not seek at Thy hands that which we have no right to ask. We make the offering and trust Thy love, O God, God our Father.

41. *In Search of Each Other*

We are aware of the circle that shuts us in—cutting us off from each other. Despite our many-sided exposure to each other we are alone in our solitariness even in the midst of the congregation. Much of our aloneness is in the nature of things; much of it is due to the uncertainties of our own feelings about ourselves and about others who make up the world of our familiars. At times, our Father, we are conscious of what we do to each other. The careless word, the unseeing look into another's face, the mood out of which all kindness is drained; these often undermine the confidence and the strength of someone who walks beside us in our journey. Preoccupied with the urgencies of our own lives we are insensitive to the ways in which we turn others away from our door empty and afraid. We cannot separate ourselves from our own hurts, our own wounds and injuries—out of the depths of our private agonies we are tempted to feel that no one understands or that those who do understand, do not care.

Thus we are in search of each other as well as of Thee in this act of worship which is our sharing. May Thy Presence invade our being until at last there begins to stir within us that which breaks the circle, spilling over into the lives of each other and we are no longer alone.

Forgive us our trespasses
As we forgive those who trespass against us.
Deliver us from evil, for Thine is the Kingdom and the Glory.

IV

Search Me,
O God!

42. Disciplined in Courage

Our Father, we are involved in the great intimacy of our own experiences, experiences that are fresh in our minds because they are still present in our lives. There are those moments when we have wrestled with some great weakness, and have failed to conquer it, but have not given up. We gather strength in this moment of love that we may pick up the struggle again when this time of prayer is over. There have been experiences in which we have been disciplined in courage and have watched our own fears mount and measure us and move in to rule and dominate our days, when out of the depths of our own spirits some new dimension of strength has come, and we have not been defeated. There is courage that is born in us as we have lived with loved ones whose burden and whose wearinesses have overtaken them in the journey. We would help but do not know how, would say the right word, but do not know what. We have sat in the silence with them until between them and us has been born a new dimension of communication and strength so that we are deeply satisfied and the load is eased; and there are those experiences that are ours because these times are ours.

These are times of great violences, times of great confusions and disorders in our own land and in the world. We do not know how to relate to these things in any way that will give a witness to our private concerns and our personal desires. We live in the midst of these things, trusting and hoping that the time will come when we will find a place at which we may register our resources, our minds, our discipline, our spirits, to the end that where there is chaos, there will be peace; where there is disorder, order; where there is bitterness and hatred, there will be love.

Thus, our Father, we offer the raw materials of our living. On Thy altar, in this moment of waiting in Thy Presence, brood over the stuff of life that we share with Thee until it becomes fully responsive to Thy Will, and our private thoughts and our private hopes and our private desires may be illumined and enlarged and become one with Thy great hopes and Thy great desires for Thy children. This is the way we feel, our Father. Accept these stirrings as our living sacrament to Thee.

69

43. Our Stubborn Wills

We are deeply conscious of our stubborn wills, the hard core of
resistance to Thy Spirit, as it would wisen our minds, make tender
our hearts, and sensitize our spirits, our Father. We want to yield
ourselves to Thee. We want to give over into Thy custody the
things that disturb us, that frighten us, that fill our days with
uneasiness and our nights with the kind of foreboding that chal-
lenges sleep and rest. This we want to do but we don't know how
to do it. Besides, we are never sure that we can trust Thee with the
things that are intimately a part of the fabric of our lives. To be rid
of them would be to expose ourselves in ways that may destroy
the kind of balance with which we function from day to day.

We wait now in Thy Presence with the silent hope that something may transpire within us that will relax the hold we have on
the things that do not make for our peace. While we wait we
remember. We remember those whose lives are a part of our own
lives in ways that are direct and sure. We would include them in
this waiting moment, but here again, our Father, we are not sure
that this is what we really want to do. We wait, that our spirits
may be clarified and our willingness may be at the disposal of the
demands of our hearts. We remember our world and all the excite-
ment of the last few days. We are troubled in our spirits because
one part of us wishes so much that we may win the race for power
and another part of us wishes so much that we may give ourselves
freely and completely to the quest for truth on the earth, in the
heavens, and in the hearts of men, and trust the decision of power
to Thee in whom at last all power finally rests. With all arrogances
put aside, with all weaknesses laid bare, with all our deep-lying
hungers exposed, we wait, our Father, for the baptism of Thy
Spirit, that we may walk confidently on the earth by the strength
of our hearts and the inspiration of Thy Spirit. If this be our por-
tion, it is enough, O God, our Father. This is enough.

44. Our Lives Are Spread Before Us

Our lives are spread before us. As we look at them, there is much that we do not recognize as belonging to us. There are those things which we see clearly and distinctly for the first time. We see how the outer edges of our lives touch the outer edges of other lives. We sense a deeper kind of relationship which gives to us the reassurance and strength we gather from those who walk the way with us. All of the predicaments, problems, and issues of our lives pile in upon us and we seek for some clue by which all of the things that involve us may fall into place and make sense to our minds and our spirits. We grapple with our hungers and desires with the fears and frustrations and overriding anxieties with which we face tomorrow and the succeeding day. We hope that some quality of stillness will invade us, that the foundation of our lives may become more secure, and the steps which we must take may be more certain and more fulfilling.

Thus, our Father, without presuming to make suggestions to Thee about what Thou shouldst do with us, and for us, we hold still with all of our lives spread before us and before Thee, with the simple trust that Thou wilt bless us. Bless us, our Father, with Thy Spirit, with Thy Wholeness, with Thy Benediction.

Beautiful

45. The God of Life

We salute the God of life. In so many little ways we have been sustained with health, and sometimes with sickness, with work to do, some of which we enjoyed and by some of which we were bored; food to eat, friends, children, elderly people, all of the little expressions of grace to keep our inadequate lives afloat. These things we finger one by one. We recall with gratitude the dreams of earlier years, all of the enthusiasm with which we looked out upon the world as we began our adventure, either as little children, or as adolescents, or as middle-aged or older persons—all of the dreams that have comforted and sustained us as we have passed through, or as we are passing through, the vicissitudes of life which sometimes seem to offer too much that casts down and depresses and so little that uplifts and inspires. We finger one by one all of the hope that we have about mankind, about peace in the world, and all of the anxiety that we have, lest in some way we may miss the road and our lives will be a nightmare rather than a joy. That this has not come to pass, we remember with thanksgiving.

We thank Thee, we thank Thee, O God, that Thou hast surrounded us with Thy love.

46. We Expose Ourselves to God

We turn aside from the tasks which consume our thoughts as we pursue our ends, to expose ourselves to the spirit of God. We offer all of the things by which we are beset as private individuals, those unique responsibilities and cares of family, all of the bewilderment of our minds because we are unable to find the answers to problems which distress, harass, and bedevil us. We offer our love, in all the curiously devious paths which that love takes, circling this one and that one, holding back from this one and that one. We offer the desire to love and the inability to know how to love. We offer all of our hostilities, those things under which we smart, for which there seems to be no relief. We offer the anger of our spirits, and the guilt of our hearts. We offer those whom we know who are sick, whose activities are suspended while they wait for the healing which seems so slow in coming, for those who have suddenly fallen upon evil moments that have wrecked their plans and desolated their hopes, torn their bodies into fragments.

All of these things we bring into the quietness as a part of ourselves which we cannot hide from Thee, O God, our Father. We have no words by which we would bend Thy will to meet our needs. We wait with confidence and trust for the movement of Thy self in all the dimensions of our being, so that we may be whole again and face what awaits us with new courage, the ceiling of our hopes lifted high.

"Let the words of my mouth, and the meditation of my heart, be acceptable in thy sight, O Lord, my strength, and my redeemer."

47. *The Pride of Our Private Lives*

We are mindful of the pride of our private lives, those moods and attitudes which tempt us to think more highly of ourselves than we ought to think; to have one scale of values by which we judge ourselves and another scale of values by which we judge our fellows. We are mindful of all the ways by which we deceive ourselves, as we find our place in the quietness before the presence of God. We would relax our minds, our spirits, our bodies, that there may float up into our awareness that which has been hidden from our thoughts because of the tensions of our daily round. We look at them with care, with diligence and integrity, seeking how we may so handle them that that which is disorderly and unclean, mean, sordid, and cheap will be purged and cleansed and purified; and that which is good, whole, upright, honest, will be reinforced and strengthened.

And thus, our Father, without pretension, we steady ourselves totally in Thy presence. Breathe through us with Thy spirit, that we may be cleansed, our Father, and forgiven!

48. We Are Deeply Agitated

Despite all of the urgencies of our private lives, despite all of the necessities by which we are surrounded day after day in the central function, in the commonplace task, our minds and our thoughts, yea, the innermost center of ourselves is deeply agitated, perturbed. We are a part this day of a momentous searching from which there can be provided no luxury of detachment. We are hurt and we are afraid. We are dazed by the relentless movement of forces which do not seem responsive to the private will and the sensitive individual judgment. We remember so many things during these times. So very many things. We seek wisdom and guidance for our own thoughts, for our own behavior. We seek wisdom and guidance for the President of our country and the leaders of the world.

We place before Thee the hard, stubborn, recalcitrant, unyielding toughness of fear and demagoguery; often the vacillating uncertainty, the weakness and the strength of goodness and righteousness; the vague, impersonal struggle that is at work in the heart of our land, dramatized in the private life and the political process. We dare to lay it bare before Thy scrutiny, O God of our spirits. Leave us not alone!

49. Our Concerns Take Shape

It is very good to wait in the presence of God and watch the concern of our private lives and our collective experiences take shape before our view. Our hearts are filled with praise and thanksgiving because we made it. We were not sure a week ago that we would. Again there is anxiety—deep, searching anxiety—not because it is not well with us, but because we feel within our spirits at the very core of our being the great sickness and distress by which our land is visited during these fateful days and fateful months. There is a great uneasiness, a sense of waiting, some dimension of quiet foreboding, some whispering of hope that dares not make itself too articulate, as we anticipate tomorrow and what it will bring in the lives of little boys and little girls, big boys and big girls, not only in Little Rock but in other parts of the country, and in other parts of the world.

We are prostrate in our guilt, uneasy in our minds. Our thoughts turn in on themselves. We do not know what to think and how to think; how to feel, what to feel. There seems to be no guidance, no voice lifted. All of this is in our minds and in our spirits.

Brooding spirit of the brooding Father, breathe into us, Thy children, the wisdom which Thou hast accumulated through the long years of anxiety which Thou hast suffered in seeing Thy children stumble, fall, rise again, trying to understand Thy will and to do Thy will. Leave us not to the desolation of our anxieties and the depths of our fears, but gentle our spirits with Thy love so that our minds may be stimulated and inspired, that what we do this day and tomorrow and tomorrow will make Thy work and the hard places where Thou dost labor a little easier. For us to do this, O God, our Father, is enough.

50. To Walk the Ordinary Path

We seek to bring together all of the fragmentation of our lives, the wide diversities of our interests, with the quiet hope that they may all be seen as one event, one experience, one life. We seek meaning for the commonplace, for the ordinary, for the nondescript; we seek strength to walk the ordinary path, to do the ordinary task; we seek wisdom to live fully, that our minds and our spirits may be filled with a quiet tranquillity, that we may walk with dignity and meaning in our way, on our street, in our home, in our tasks, by the light in our hearts and by the light in the sky.

We ask of Thee, O God, no miracles, no vast upturning of life in startling dimensions; we seek simple assurance that will absorb the weariness of the daily round, that will give lift to the ordinary way, confident, our Father, that Thou art very close to us, closer than breathing. Tutor us, that we may trust Thy nearness and be lifted up and strengthened.

51. Fresh Manifestations of Grace

We remember those experiences in which we have been overwhelmed by a fresh manifestation of the grace, the care, and the love of God. Our hearts have voiced their thanks and their praise. We are mindful of the ways by which we have felt sorry for things that we have done, and how we have wished that we could undo them and give to ourselves, and those involved with us, the fresh start and the new beginning. We remember those about whom and for whom we have cares and anxieties; those who are sick, who find in the days that seem to stretch out before them no turning in the road; those whose needs have somehow come through to us, and we would help but we do not know how. We remember them, as we gather in our own spirits before God.

We turn without pretension and without self-praise or pride to Thee, our Father. Search our spirits, leave no stone unturned in our yards, that there may be nothing hidden from Thee by our will or our plan or our devices. It brings such relief to us to be able to let down our bars in Thy presence, and to think and feel with freedom and without inhibition, under Thy scrutiny and surrounded by Thy love. Accept our lives as they are, our Father, and grant that in this acceptance we may be healed, strengthened, renewed, and redeemed.

52. Free of Carking Care

There is the natural longing within us for a life free of carking cares, the insistent urgencies of the unpleasant task or the handicap of mind, spirit, emotions, or body; the great desire to be rid of whatever there is that slows down, that encumbers, that makes more difficult the journey which is set before us. These things surround us as we settle into the quietness of prayer. Each one has his own private collection. We seek how we may be able so to detach ourselves from them that we let them be in the silence in the presence of God. There are ancient anxieties, time-wearied weaknesses, uncontrollable and explosive temper, scar tissue from old injuries, the troubled feeling that we can never quite define, our reaction to the impact of the age of violence in which we live.

We want to be rid of that which comes between us and Thy vision, our Father. Teach us how. We are but little children fumbling in the darkness. Do not reject even our weakness, O God, but accept us totally as we are. Work over us and knead us and fashion us, until at last we take on the character which is Thy Spirit and the mind which is Thy Mind. We trust Thee to do Thy Thing in us, O God, the Father of our spirits.

53. Moments of the Past

Our Father, we are constanly amazed and often startled by the miracle of our own lives. We remember moments of the past in which, in some strange and wonderful way, we were delivered from something that threatened, something that would have destroyed or hurt or injured us, and we give to Thee the after-praise of our hearts. When we are most ourselves we remember to do the thing that not only seems to our minds to be right, true, genuine, and authentic, but to do the thing which brings into our whole being a sense of peace, a sense of health and one-ness. We are troubled, our Father, by the divisions that are within us, the deep conflicts in our own spirits which cause us to be at war within, which cause us to be a house divided against itself. This sense of inner conflict and division is a part of the larger conflict and division that exist among Thy children everywhere. The peace which we seek in our private lives, that we may be one thing, is a part of the peace that we seek for all Thy children, that they may be one family in Thy presence, living in Thy world. How to do this, how to experience this? If we but knew with all our being, dost Thou think then we would try?

Out of Thy long experience with life that Thou hast created, the ups and downs of the journey of life by which Thou hast sought to make beauty out of ugliness and harmony out of dis-harmony, wholeness out of things that are deep in their division, hast Thou learned so much that the overflow of Thy wisdom might be shared by us? That we too may know how to win beauty out of ugliness, peace out of confusion, order out of chaos?

"How precious are thy thoughts unto me, O God! how great is the sum of them! . . . Search me, O God, and know my heart; try me, and know my thoughts; And see if there be any wicked way in me, and lead me in the way everlasting."

80

54. The Barrenness of Our Lives

A curse on him who relies on man,
    and leans upon mere human aid,
turning his thoughts from the Eternal!
He is like some desert scrub,
    that never thrives,
set in a dry place in the steppes,
    in a salt, solitary land.
But happy he who relies on the Eternal,
    with the Eternal for his confidence!
He is like a tree planted beside a stream,
    reaching its roots to the water;
untouched by any fear of scorching heat,
    its leaves are ever green,
it goes on bearing fruit in days of drought,
    and lives serene.

It is so easy, our Father, for us to say those words. Even in the saying of them there are moments when we sense our identity with them, but the conflict in our spirits goes so deep. There is something so reassuring and confident and visible about the strength, the presence, the activity of man, something we can understand and touch, something that is flesh of our flesh and bone of our bone and mind of our mind. There is something so mysterious and sometimes so distant, our Father, when we use the words about Thee. They seem empty or so full of meaning that we are devastated and made desolate by the barrenness of our own lives in contrast. But beneath the conflict, beneath the churning, turmoil, and turbulence we sense something more; if we could just hold it against all that divides and separates, if we could just hold it in weakness and strength, in sin and in righteousness; if we could just hold it against the despair of our spirits, or against the soaring height of our dreams, O God. We do want to know Thy presence and feel the movement of Thy spirit at our depths. We do hunger for the cleansing of Thy grace. Wilt Thou take unto Thyself our hearts' desiring and wilt Thou follow along all of its courses, until at last we are in Thee and Thou art in us? Above all else this speaks to our condition, O God.

55. *The Particulars of Our Lives*

We bring into the quietness of Thy presence, our Father, all the particulars of our lives. We would not hold back from Thy scrutiny any facet of ourselves, the things of which we are ashamed and by which our spirits are embarrassed; the good things which we have done and the good impulses of which we are aware; those whom we recognize by ties of kinship but with whom we have no fellowship, those whom we recognize by ties of kinship but with whom we have deep and abiding fellowship; those whom we love as best we can, those whom we have not learned yet how to want to love; the quiet satisfaction of some part of us that is found in the strength of hostility and the reinforcement of bitterness of heart. Our maladies we bring before Thee: the things in our bodies that have given us trouble and we cannot quite shake off despite all of the skills of the minds of men and all the wisdom of the art of healing; those deep and turbulent upheavals in our spirits that keep our minds divided and our emotions in revolt.

Into the quietness, our Father, we bring all of the facets of our lives. We hold them there, trying to restrain ourselves, lest we ask of Thee that which is not in accordance with Thy purpose and Thy will, waiting that we may discern the movement of Thy spirit amidst all of the hinterland of our region. Of all the peoples of the world and all the troubled places, we bring before Thee this morning the turbulent, pain-racked, suffering spirit of Algeria. After more than a hundred leaden-footed days and months and years, our Father, this day they will speak with freedom what it is in their hearts to say as Thy children. Brood over that troubled land, to the end that some way may be found for the great healing, for forgiveness of Frenchmen and Moslem. O God, do not despair of us, do not despair of us, but hold us with Thy love, until we learn how to love, O God, our Father.

56. The Meaning of Our Own Lives

Our Father, we gather ourselves together in all of our available parts to see if somehow there may be made clear for us the meaning of our own lives and the meaning of the journey to which we are committed. We confess our sins, as we wait in Thy presence, those things within us of which we are grossly ashamed, those things within us and those expressions of our lives of which we are scarcely aware until our spirits are sensitized by Thy spirit, things which do violence to Thy purposes and Thy will for us and our world. We want to be better than we are. So often we do not know how. Again and again we are moved by the impulse to be better than we are but we do not quite know how to give way to it, that it might sweep through us with its renewal and its inspiration. We are such divided, tempest-tossed, driven children. If we knew the right words to say, our Father, we would say them, if somehow we could bring our minds and our hearts into focus so that what we mean we say, and what we say we do. If we could do this, it would help us to be whole. Shall we seek to make peace within ourselves by the ordering of our wills in accordance with Thy will, or shall we seek to help those about us whose needs are great and in helping them perhaps find wholeness for ourselves? What shall we do, our Father?

Oh, that we might be unanimous within ourselves, that our total being and our lives might be a tuned instrument in Thy hands, making the kind of music that would calm the distressed, that would heal the broken body and mind, that would bring tenderness to those who feel rejected and outcast. As we wait in Thy presence, our Father, gather us in, that we might be a lung through which Thy spirit may breathe. Is this asking too much? We wait, O God our Father, we wait.

57. Some Centering Moment

We wait in the quietness for some centering moment that will redefine, reshape, and refocus our lives. It does seem to be a luxury to be able to give thought and time to the ups and downs of one's private journey while the world around is so sick and weary and desperate. But, our Father, we cannot get through to the great anxieties that surround us until, somehow, a path is found through the little anxieties that beset us. Dost Thou understand what it is like to be caught between the agony of one's own private needs and to be tempest-tossed by needs that overwhelm and stagger the mind and paralyze the heart? Dost Thou understand this, our Father?

For the long loneliness, the deep and searching joy and satisfaction, the boundless vision—all these things that give to Thee so strong a place in a world so weak—we thank Thee, Father. For whatever little grace Thou wilt give to Thy children even as they wait in confidence and stillness in Thy presence, we praise Thee. O love of God, love of God, where would we be without Thee? Where?

58. Mindful of Our Weaknesses

Our minds are full of the private intensity of our own lives, the ways in which, despite all of our efforts, so many of the dreams which we cherish do not seem to find fulfillment in the experiences of life as we know them. We are mindful of our weaknesses, the things which we have tried to overcome for so long a time, and yet which dog our footsteps and never seem to lose the scent of our trail; the goodness which we sometimes sense as belonging to our natures and our spirits, which moves in and out of our lives like some fleeting ghost with no resting place. We remember those whose responsibilities are so much greater than ours, on whose shoulders rest the fateful decisions which will make the big difference for so many of us who regard ourselves of no particular moment—those managers of the common life, those in whose hands rest authority and dominion and yet who wrestle even as we wrestle with the weakness that will never lose the trail.

And so, our Father, we come to Thee, feeling the presence of those others whose ways we cannot know, whose temptations we cannot understand. And Thy children, our Father, seek for the light to illumine the path against the darkness. We do this, that Thy will, Thy purpose, Thy love will reign in our hearts and in the great outer world in which we live and move and struggle and suffer and enjoy.

59. *The Hurt of Isolation*

So much of our common life is spent in seeking ways by which we may break the isolation and solitariness and loneliness of the individual life. There is within us the hunger for companionship and understanding, for the experience of free and easy access to the life of another, so that in the things which we must face, the enemies with which we must do battle, we shall not be alone. Sometimes this isolation is brought about because life has eliminated from our world, one by one, those who have won the right to companion us on our journey. Sometimes the isolation is due to evil things which we have done deliberately or against our conscious wills, rendering those around us afraid and injured, and we are alone. Sometimes the isolation is due to a demand which our hearts make upon ourselves—the right to be free from involvements, the right to experience detachment, the right to take the long, hard look in solitariness and in isolation. But whatever may be the cause, it is so very good to sense the common character of our quest and the mutual support by which we are sustained.

We thank Thee, our Father, that this is so. Thy rod and Thy staff they comfort us and we thank Thee, O God; we thank Thee, our Father.

60. *Events That Imprison*

Our common life is lived under the shadow of the event that imprisons and encumbers; the sin that opens up always dimensions of forgiveness that we have not explored; the temptations that are conquered and must be reconquered over and over and over; the grief that silently gnaws away at all the dreams and hopes and simple plans and far-flung ambitions of the common life, grief that finds no solace in all the ways that we have tried; the fear of tomorrow and what it may bring, the fear of disease that cripples and lays waste and despoils and outrages the dignity of the self. We live under the shadow of the event, and our hearts reach out for some measure of release and relief, hoping that our desires are not in vain.

And so, our Father, it is with overwhelming relief that we come into Thy presence and expose ourselves to Thee and witness in utter amazement how Thy spirit transcends the event and turns the shadow into life. For this we rejoice and give to Thee the emptying of our cup of thanksgiving. This is so good, Our Father, and we thank Thee for just this swirling moment of freedom.

61. Experience of Self-confidence

It is one of the special graces of life that each of us can rely upon his own strength to do so many things for himself and for others. The quiet sense of assurance and independence is so strengthening to the heart and to the spirit. Sometimes our experience of self-confidence is so overwhelming that we forget the limitations by which our lives are surrounded. There are so many things to which we are heirs that are not the result of any act of our own, any wisdom which we have distilled, any kind of knowledge which has been vouchsafed to our minds. Always we are surrounded by so much more than we are: so much more wisdom, so much more understanding, so much more knowledge, so much more caring, so much more love, so much more mercy.

As we remember this in our meditation, we find new tongues of praise to give to Thee, O God, for Thy brooding care beyond which despite arrogance and pride and independence and self-confidence, we cannot drift. Gather then unto Thyself, O God, these spirits of ours, that they may come to themselves in Thee; and this, this will suffice, this will suffice even us, O God, God of our spirits.

62. *The Presence of the Fact*

Our spirits and our minds stand at attention in the presence of the fact, which is our little life. Our days are crowded by events, sometimes cruel, sometimes heartless, sometimes meaningless, sometimes full of joy and richness. We finger them one by one in Thy presence, our Father—the grief that we have known that lingers long after the moment of its first great wild tearing at the fibers of the heart; the anguish we have felt because the thing for which we have worked so long and so hard, that into which we have poured so much of the living stuff of our days, has turned sour in our spirits or become whitened ashes in our hands and we are bereft; the temptations that have been our daily companions from our youth and which, through all the leaden-footed months and years of our living, we have not found a way to escape; the great resolutions of our spirits that stirred in us at other times, sending us on a joyful journey, questing, full of confidence that life would hold in its hands that which we wrought with all of our passionate endeavor. We sit now in the quietness before Thee, having not found it.

O God, God our Father, hold us in the sweep of Thy hands under the shadow of Thy wing, until at last all of our anguish dies and our fears are removed, and the joy of Thy spirit possesses our lives. Thus we may know for ourselves this day and tomorrow and tomorrow, not only that Thou canst be trusted, our Father, but that life itself can be counted on. With this assurance we can stand anything that life can do to us; without this assurance our souls are desolate, it is night, and we are afraid.

63. The Assessment of One's Life

It is no ordinary thing to undertake the assessment of one's life, to take the backward look over the way that one has come, and to remember. To remember how it was with oneself a year ago—with what hopes and enthusiasms and visions one greeted the beginning of the year. Or to remember how one dragged one's feet into the year, and how as the months moved into view many things changed so that there is in some of our hearts quiet rejoicing that life has fallen for us in easy places. For some others there is the simple anguish that comes from the frustrations which were unanticipated, which had to be endured, and there is left a residue of weariness and heartache for which there does not seem to be any solace or any comfort. It is good to be here and to feel our way into each other's presence, each other's experiencing, each other's heart and mind, and in that feeling to sense the strength which comes from the shoulder that touches and the heart that cares.

We remember, God of our spirits, all of those in the world who have no place of refuge either in the hearts of others or under the roofs of others. We remember those who stand at the places of power, who carry within the sweep of their gestures the life and death of generations yet unborn.

Leave Thy world, O God, not alone in the logic of its life, but love us still, even as we break Thy heart and drive Thy mind to distraction. O love of God, love of God, leave us not to the fulfillment of the devices of our minds but be with us as we pace ourselves through the valleys and the shadows of our many dyings.

64. Private World of Burdens

We have no flow of words, our Father, by which we would ingratiate ourselves to Thee. We come each with his private world of burdens and cares and joys and sorrows, of righteousness and unrighteousness, of weakness and strength, bringing with us those things of which we are very proud and those things which shame our hearts and turn our spirits inside out. We bring our concern for the sick, those whose names we remember who have worked long and hard and who stand within reach of the fulfillment of a lifetime of striving and who are stricken with disease for which the mind of man can find no answer. All whom we love and who love us, we bring and place before Thee with all the imperfections by which we relate to them. We do not ask anything of Thee, our Father; we make our offering of everything and let it rest in Thy presence. For us, O God, this is sufficient.

65. Reach Us in Our Weakness

We are mindful of the ways by which we have come to Thee. For some the journey has been through many paths and bypaths, leading sometimes one place and other times to another place. But always the hunger persists: that there is a meaning in life that is greater than the meaning we are experiencing, a depth of feeling more profound than anything that we know, a way of thinking that transcends the furthest rims of our own thoughts. It is good, therefore, to feel our minds and spirits gentled by a wider circle of meaning and thought than anything that we have known before, and to know, each after the pattern of his own need, that Thou art our Father, nearer than breathing, closer than hands and feet. The thought is too much for us; the assurance is more than we can abide.

Reach us, our Father, in our weakness, in our sin, in our failure, and in our pride, that we may know that we are Thy children and that Thou art our Father.

66. To Acknowledge the Need for Strength

It is so much easier to acknowledge the need for strength than it is to discover resources for strength. It is so much easier to acknowledge the need for courage than to do the things needful for the courageous stand. It is so much easier to acknowledge the need for forgiveness than to quell one's pride and humble one's heart and seek forgiveness.

Thus, our Father, with the thoughts of our minds we try to prepare the way for the entering of Thy spirit into our conscious feelings and our conscious reflections; but these words seem so empty, so hollow, so raucous, so noisy. We wait, doing what we can to abide the silence, hoping that there may be such deep stillness within us that Thou mayest enter, blending with the landscape of our spirits, transforming and making all new and refreshed as if it were a change that we wrought in ourselves. O God, for Thy vast humility we utter the praise of our silence and we thank Thee, our Father.

67. *Floating Hopes*

Each of us is mindful of the tight circle in which his life is lived; all of the ways by which life closes in, stultifies, frightens, disturbs; all of those private regions of the heart where desires have their beginnings, the quiet anxieties of the spirit that express themselves in many ways that defeat the outward life. We remember the floating hopes and dreams and desires that surround us but do not quite take hold upon us.

As we still ourselves in Thy presence, O God, our Father, we trust that there may be visited upon us that which can widen the narrowness of our little lives, that which can make room within us for love where there now is hate, for understanding where there is misunderstanding, for courage where there is fear. We want this so much for ourselves. We are tired, our Father, of the narrowness and the weariness and the littleness of our lives. This we know, but again and again, our Father, we do not know how to go any other way. We try. Thou knowest it. Now we wait, we wait with confidence, that what we have been unable to do, using all the powers of our minds and imaginations, Thou mayest show us how to do as we wait in Thy presence. O God of our spirits, we await Thy pleasure.

68. The Real—The Unreal

We are baffled again and again by the way in which life seems to present us with the real as over against the unreal. We find it hard to know what to us is the real. Is it the tangible, the concrete, the familiar? Is it that which we possess, the possession of which gives to us power and strength to carry on our private enterprises? Is it our hopes and ambitions? Is it our fears and our desperations? Is it the thing we say or is it the thing we mean by what we say?

We thank Thee, our Father, that, surrounded as we are by so much that changes and shifts and rearranges itself, Thou dost speak to us with assurance and with constancy, deep within the central place of our own hearts. It is for this that we rejoice, that despite all of the confusion and chaos around us and within us, it is still possible to hear the whisper of Thy voice in our hearts. To hear this, O God, our Father, is to live today and forever.

69. Our Longings and Our Hopes

We are constantly reminded that our lives move out in many directions, carrying in their weight the burden of our thoughts, our concerns, our dreams, our hopes, our longings. It is as if the dreams, the hopes, the longings of mankind roamed the earth, finding wherever they may a response in hearts and minds, far removed, speaking other tongues, their roots watered by other faiths. We are mindful that we are surrounded by a great multitude of longings, yearnings, and aspirations that knock quietly at the doors of our own spirits, seeking from us a kind of help that only the sensitive mind or the kind heart can give.

We know somewhat concerning our own longings and yearnings. We know what it is like to lay claim to the strength of our heritage and the guidance of our own faith. We know what it is like to share in the common worship, caught up by the sweep of our own religious tradition. We know the comfort of the familiar landscape that enables us to find our way even in the darkness of our sin and sorrow.

Teach us, our Father, to know the yearnings and the longings of those of other lands who call Thee by a strange name, who find a community of worship in practices far removed from what in our self-righteousness we would regard as either sacred or holy, who find in their heritage that which gives strength to their footsteps and whose lives are gathered into transcendent meaning by the glow of their own religious tradition. How hard it is for us to affirm with all our hearts that Thou hast not left Thyself without specific witness in every land, in every age, with every people!

Hold us secure as with great trepidation of heart we would learn of Thee in ways unfamiliar and in melodies alien to our ears.

70. The Act of Confession

It is good to confess in the quietness whatever there is within us that cries out for confession and to feel in the act of confession that He who hears and judges also understands and loves. It is no ordinary thing to be free enough within to confess, even to God, that which cries out for confession. It is wonderful beyond measure to be able to share the stirrings of thanksgiving which we feel and to do this with the kind of confidence that makes it unnecessary to custom-make the language that we use . . . To be able to say thanks to God, with no necessity to try to impress Him with our thoughtfulness or to store up some form of merit that will plead our case at other times when gratitude is lacking and thanksgiving is far removed.

It is no ordinary thing simply to say to Thee, O God, thank you so much, thank you so very much, our Father.

71. We Shall Content Ourselves

Our Father, we do not have the words by which we can express to Thee either the joy which is ours or the hopes or yearnings that we have for ourselves and for the world as we set forth on our way into the future. We shall content ourselves then, our Father, by exposing to Thy scrutiny and Thy love all that is within us, the most private and personal thoughts that we have, the most intimate yearnings and longings and ambitions, the deep purple cast of our fears and our anxieties, the tender uncertainties which envelop us as we think about what it is that we most want to do and be and experience in these months ahead. We lay bare before Thee our lives without disguise, without sentimentality, without pretension, but utterly as we are. Hold us close that we may see ourselves through Thine eyes, that we may sense what it is that Thou art trying to do in this world grown old and weary, with so much that breaks the heart and unroofs the reason. Hold us, our Father, until we sense through the grain of our being what it is that Thou wouldst have us be and do in our way, where we are, that the contemplation of Thy world will give to Thee some measure of comfort and satisfaction.

Oh, to be no hindrance to Thy will. Oh, to be the lung through which Thou canst breathe. Oh, to be this would be all, our Father.

72. The Privilege of Pause

It is a very great and intimate privilege to be able to pause, to turn aside from the things that occupy and preoccupy the mind in the daily round, to wait on the threshold of a new week and to look back over the week that has passed. From this vantage point we see perhaps more clearly than the experiences themselves could have indicated the meaning of so many things which affected us and which we affected during the week that has passed: the strong word we used when the impulse was to be silent; the moment of misunderstanding when we turned our gaze away from the truth to embrace the lie in which we found comfort and reassurance; the deed which we performed when even before the task was complete we knew it was but a poor representation of the integrity of our intent. All of the hours of the days move before us as we stand looking back over the way we have come.

We anticipate tomorrow, some of us with high hopes and abiding enthusiasms, some of us with anxiety that deepens as the hours of a new day approach, some with fear lest the decisions that must be made be decisions that are in themselves self-defeating, denying the quality of meaning which we have distilled out of the years of our living.

We anticipate tomorrow, our Father, not because it is our promise and our due but because there is within us a deep yearning for the fulfillment of that which we have not known before, for the opportunity to be what, if we have another chance, we think we may become. Brood over us as we stand on the threshold, giving to our faltering footsteps the sturdiness that can only come from One for whom tomorrow and today and yesterday are but one moment in a vast series of moments. Make tender our spirits that we may not through any callousness of mind or hardness of heart hurt and maim and injure where we could bless and cure and heal. Leave us not alone to the independence of our minds or to the hardness of our minds and spirits, but surround us with Thy caring, that what we do will be what we mean and what we say will be inspired by the integrity of the intent.

73. Our Words Seem Empty and Barren

The words which we would utter before Thee seem so empty and barren of what we feel and sense that we would delight our spirits by being silent before Thee. We remember so many things as we wait in Thy presence: the good which we achieved when we were not really intent upon the doing of the good deed; and the good that we did not achieve when we were so intent upon the quality of the good deed that we were sure of its effect and its integrity. We remember these things as we wait. We remember the dreams that we have had at various stages in our lives. Some we followed for a season and then abandoned. Some others we followed until we discovered that they had abandoned us. And now as we wait in Thy presence we wonder about them. We search our spirits to see if there is still lurking within the unfulfilled reaches of our minds and aspirations some goal to which we may respond which will bring into even these days that are upon us the strength and the fullness and the vitality which up and down the years we have sought.

We would not close our minds, our Father, to the concerns that are on the periphery of our thought: the concerns for disarmament; for the settling of the long bloody turmoil through which France and Algeria have fought in the darkness. If we were wise enough, our Father, we would yield our concern for ourselves to Thy concern on our behalf. But before the thoughts take shape in our minds, all that they do not say, all that they cannot grasp, all that they cannot mean is so terribly clear to us as we wait, that the thoughts die aborning and we can only trust that there is in Thy great heart the concern for our well-being that will steady us through the days and the nights and the journeyings of Thy children on this planet. What we hope for all Thy children, very quietly we seek for ourselves. We do long so much to be better than we are, to be kinder than we have ever been, to love, God, to love.

74. Thou Preparest a Table

"Thou preparest a table before me in the presence of mine enemies; thou anointest my head with oil; my cup runneth over. Surely goodness and mercy shall follow me all the days of my life; and I will dwell in the house of the Lord for ever."

The moving touch of Thy spirit is upon us, O God, inspiring us on many levels of gratitude for the graces that so abundantly Thou dost bestow upon us: The gift of our mind, always seeking and probing and searching, always trying to understand the vast conglomerates of our experiences and our lives. The grace of our bodies and the miracle that they represent to each of us. All of the intimate processes by which health is sustained and by which recovery from illness is made possible. The gift of the spirit that is within us—we do not quite understand, our Father, the way in which it moves us at levels deeper than the mind and deeper than the understanding, the strange journeys upon which it sends us, and all of the little breaths of awareness that it makes possible as we move day by day in the pilgrimage which is our private way. We are grateful for all the ties by which we are held in our place —ties that reach back into childhood and family; ties that are in the hands of those around us who love us and who trust us and who believe in us; those wider ties that stabilize the common life and that give to our days structure and meaning so that the things that we do each day are seen by us as being a part of a larger whole, bringing into our little life the big meaning and the great vision.

We are overwhelmed, our Father, by the graces of life and all the ways by which Thou dost lavish Thyself upon us. Teach us in the quietness of this waiting moment how we may so relate, so become a part of Thy beneficence that we shall become kind human beings, tender human beings, thoughtful and gracious human beings, giving to all of life, as we move, a benediction breathing peace. O God, accept our thanks, our very personal thanks.

75. We Don't Know How

We find it very difficult, our Father, to bring to a point of focus all of the fragmentation and divisiveness of our lives. We ask Thee to draw upon Thy long experience with Thy children, and out of this special wisdom and understanding, to interpret the words which we say to Thee in our prayer. We are overwhelmed by our great inability somehow to manage the imperfections of life, the imperfections of our own private lives, the clear insight which suddenly becomes dim and often disappears at the moment when we are sure that we could act upon it; the good deed which we express and which, as it leaves us, wings on its way to fulfill itself in another's life, in another's need. And as we watch, we are horrified at the way in which something goes wrong and the good deed is not a good deed in the way in which it works, and we are thrown back upon ourselves. We don't know how to manage the imperfections of our lives, the imperfections of so many expressions of our lives.

We have brooded over nature. We have understood here and there some of its inner mandates, and we have been able to translate these mandates into expressions of machinery and objects, and we have learned how to operate these machines and to make these objects, created out of our insights, expressions of our intent. We have made these things into servants to obey our minds and our wills and then, suddenly, we are faced with radical and quick and devastating breakdown! Something goes wrong, we do not know what, and there is mindless violence and destruction. We don't know how to manage the imperfections of our lives.

Now we wait for the fateful moment when once again we ourselves as a nation will begin learning, with more finesse and accuracy, to kill, to destroy. And we feel, some of us, that the only way to survive is to do this, and some of us are sure that this is but to hasten the end of the age.

How to manage the imperfections of our minds and our spirits, our thoughts, even our intent? O God, we don't know how. We don't know how. We don't know how. Take all the outcry of our anguish, all the sin and brokenness of our faltering selves and hold them with such sureness that we learn from Thee.

76. The Hasty Word

We have turned aside from the tasks and the duties and the responsibilities which involve us day after day to present ourselves with as much confidence and faith as we can muster, hoping that in Thy presence and in the great quietness of this waiting moment we might find the measure of deep and inner peace without which the enterprise of our private lives cannot be fulfilled. We share with Thee all of the meaning that we have been able to garner out of the days of our living. We see as if by a flash of blinding light the meaning of something which we have done; the hasty word, the careless utterance, the deliberate act by which another was injured or confused, the decision to do what even at the time we felt was neither the right thing nor the thing which we were willing to back with our lives. All of these things crowd in upon us, our Father. We want to be sure that what we say in Thy presence and what we feel in Thy presence will be honest and clear and sincere. As we look at this aspect of our lives, there is only one moving request which we make and that is for forgiveness: forgiveness for the sin, for the wrong act, for the bad deed; forgiveness, our Father. We do not know altogether what it is that we want beyond this. We see our lives, the goals which we have set for ourselves. And as we wait now in the quietness, these goals are weighted or held in tender balance before Thy scrutiny and Thy caring, and we see them in a new light. And we trust that somehow as we move into the tasks that await us, the radiance which we sense now will cast a long glow to guide us in tomorrow's darkness.

We are mindful also of all kinds of needs in the world. Those needs which are close at hand and about which we have had some superficial concern, which we have met casually out of the richness of our own sense of surplus. There are other needs at which we have not dared to look, our Father, because we fear what our response to such needs might make us do or become lest we find all of the careful plans of our lives upset and the goals which we have put in focus thrown out of line or discarded, because as we look into the depths of certain needs we cannot ever be ourselves in happiness and peace again; this is too costly for us. Yet, our Father, as we wait here, these needs move before us. We hear the cry and the anguish of the destitute, of the hungry, of the hopeless, of the despairing. We cannot be deaf, but we don't know what to do. We don't know how to give and not destroy ourselves. O God, deal with our disorder with redemptive tenderness so that we, as we live our tomorrows, may not be ashamed of Thy grace that has made our lives move in such tranquil places. These are all the words we have. Take them and let them say to Thee the words of our hearts and our spirits.

77. Walls of Disappointment

When trapped by walls of disappointment and tempted to panic by disordered thinking, calmness is the only solution for men, for the acts of Providence are so hidden it is hard to understand how delicate are the influences emanating from our own mind. There are great changes that come about in the darkest hours where there is no hope and the encircling gloom is terrifying to the heart. It is difficult to understand the power at that moment. Calmness in the midst of chaos, serenity in the midst of feverish activity, are the secret that all commanders must know, the secret revealed in crisis, that the soul that is calm with controlled emotion is performing an act of faith. To do this we must remember our way back into the very center of our being, to that eternal fountain of refreshment within. Otherwise we block, frustrate, and delay, giving over to a frantic spirit and a mind gutted with panic. It is a hard lesson; perhaps it should be an easy one.

Consider: you believe that you are a child of God. You have a vision, however vague, of your own sense of godhood. Your bewildered, tired, impatient self can only glimpse this in moments far between as you conceive time. But what is a week, a month, yea, even a year? In the deep, inner quietness of your spirit, time stands still—before and after are lost in now, there is no movement, no action, even the outer edges of awareness blend into the surrounding calm.

It is this calmness that now you must carry with you into the maelstrom of your hectic days. Let it be a remembered grace and a nourishing companion. And this is enough!

78. Our Little World

It is so comforting to be preoccupied with ourselves, our needs, and all that those needs indicate in terms of the behavior of our lives; our own dreams to which, in the silence, we may give wings, with the hope that their stirring flight may bring to our leaden feet a lighter movement, a quicker step. It is so reassuring and comforting to be preoccupied with our little world and all the things that go to make it pulse and beat and throb.

We tear ourselves away from such preoccupation as we wait in the silence before God. For in addition to ourselves there are others far removed from us by land and sea and air, by cultures and civilizations and faiths and religions, who must be gathered in to sit beside us in the quietness. Those of us who live in countries where the fever is high, where violence walks up and down the street and is the companion of all the retreats of the human spirit. . . . Those who are denied food and shelter through no merit or demerit of their own but whose lives are cast in hard and barren and arid places. . . . Those lonely watchmen on the towers of our time, the prophets who speak and those who dare not speak, the statesmen who agonize, seeking some answer to the riddle by which their days are surrounded and their aspirations choked and stifled. . . .

All of those who have a broad and deep sense of responsibility for the total life, we bring *them* to sit beside us in the quietness. And, O God, as we share our spirits with their spirits, gather us in by Thy love and understanding so that we shall have a new faith in life and the great dread that hangs over us about tomorrow will be seen, penetrated, and transcended. If by some little grace so great a benediction is ours, we give the quiet, muted praise of our distracted hearts, O God, our Father.

79. *Always Making Decisions*

Always, I am making decisions. There are some decisions that are deliberately negative. They cut across everything in me that is positive and affirming. They may involve much or little as far as my immediate destiny is concerned. It is a crucial thing to come to a point of decision, to weigh causes of action, to sense the meaning of direction. It is in such a moment that man knows whether he is on the side of life or death, and the choice is his to make. To affirm life is to accept growth, to accept challenge, to move with all of one's full-orbed intent in response to the deepest that stirs within. Then the miracle takes place. The deepest thing in man somehow makes contact with the deepest things in life, and he knows that the decision is right, that the decision is on the side of life and not death. Of course, a life-giving decision may be difficult. It may cause much heartache and disturbance, even upheaval, but the issue is never in doubt. It is a terrible thing to make a decision which one knows, somewhere in the profound recesses of one's being, is against life.

Teach us to overcome our fear of life and in that freedom may we learn to understand life and in our understanding of life, to love life. Steady us, our Father, that we may cast our vote for life and not against life.

"Let the words of my mouth and the meditation of my heart be acceptable in thy sight, O Lord, my rock and my redeemer."

80. Our Private World of Concern

It is not easy to look deeply into our own lives. As we do so there is much that we see that we do not understand—some deeds that are clear to us but the reason behind them, the motives for them, elude us. The widening gulf between the intent and the fulfillment yawns in a manner that stirs the heart with panic and anxiety. The good we see to do and the good we shrink from doing often sit in judgment upon our days. Such judgment stirs our hearts with a sense of weakness and despair. We remember some moments from the past when our lives were watched over by a guardian angel that came between us and the full-orbed consequences of our deeds. We remember that we were somhow rescued without merit and without desert when we were caught in the grapple of some persistent temptation. We look long and hard at the multiple graces by which the pattern of our lives has been structured, pointed, focused, and reassured. All of these things and many others pile in upon us when we are surrounded as now by a climate in which so much has taken place for so many, for so long.

For this dimension of awareness we pour out the great mixture of our lives before Thee for Thy benediction and Thy blessing, O God, God of our spirits.

81. Witness in Our Spirits

It is good to remember that God has not left Himself without a witness in our spirits, that despite all of the wanderings of our footsteps, despite all of the ways by which we have sought to circumvent His truth within us, despite all of the weaknesses of spirit and of mind and of resoluteness and of body, despite all of the blunders by which we have isolated ourselves from our fellows and proven unworthy of the love and the trust and the confidence by which again and again our faltering lives are surrounded, despite all of this, it is good to remember that God has not left Himself without a witness in our lives.

Deliberately we turn, therefore, to Thee, our Father, to lay bare our secret, waiting for the penetration of Thy light within us, that we may be healed and forgiven and confirmed anew, to the end that we may walk in Thy way and live in Thy light. We thank Thee, our Father, that Thou hast not left us alone to the devices of our minds and our spirits, but within us and about us there is Thy witness, and for this we rejoice to give to Thee the thanks of our hearts, this day.

82. The Sustainer of Life

It is of enormous reassurance to us, our Father, that Thou art the sustainer and the holder of life, that despite all of our own limitations and finitudes, despite all our weaknesses and failures, despite all of the soarings of our minds and imaginations and our spirits, always we come back to the deeply-lying assurance that Thou art the sustainer of life, the holder of all creation, and the guarantor of all our values. This is of such overwhelming reassurance to us that we celebrate in simple words of praise this almighty grace.

We offer on our part not merely the good deeds of which we are aware at times, not merely the concerns for our fellows which sometimes lead us to simple deeds or glorious acts of self-sacrifice, but we offer Thee the things that we might become—all of the possibilities of our lives, the potentials not yet realized. We offer to Thee our failures also; those times when something breaks down and we do not know what, or when something breaks down and we do know what; all that we might have been at a particular time and were not; all of the sense of conscience that disturbs and whips and tortures because we have not been in quality and in kind what we knew at the time we could have been in quality and kind. And beyond all of these expressions of ourselves, our Father, we offer to Thee ourselves. This is what we want to do, and sometimes we are able to do it—just to say to Thee, Father, here am I. My life as it is at its depth I give to Thee. And I want Thee to hold it so that it is no longer my life to do with in accordance with my whims, my impulses, my desires, or even my needs, but to take my life and to hold it until it takes on Thy character, Thy mind, Thy purposes. If Thou wilt do this and if Thou wilt help me to do this, then I can be in myself what is truest and surest in me. And this, O God, is all, all, all.

83. *Thou Dost Not Become Weary*

It is our faith and our confidence, our Father, that Thou dost not become weary, because always before Thee we present the same sorry spectacle. It is our trust that Thou dost not get tired of us but that always Thou dost remain constant, even as we do not; that Thou dost remain true even when we take refuge in falsehood and error; that Thou dost remain kind and gracious when our hearts are hard and callous; that Thy scrutiny and Thy judgment hold despite all of our whimpering, self-pity, and shame. It is so good to have this kind of assurance and to know, as we move into the days and the hours that are still left to us, that we are not alone but that we are comforted and straightened by Thy brooding presence.

We would ask forgiveness for our sins, but of so much that is sinful in us we have no awareness. We would seek to offer to Thee the salutation of our spirits and our minds were we able to tear ourselves away from preoccupation with our own concerns, our own anxieties, our own little lives. We would give to Thee the "nerve center" of our consent if for one swirling moment we could trust Thee to do with us what our lives can stand.

O God, our Father, take the chaos and confusion and disorder of our minds and spirits and hold them so completely in Thy grasp that the impure thing will become pure, the crooked thing will become straight, and the crass and hard thing will be gentled by Thy spirit. Oh, that we may have the strength to see and the vision to comprehend what in us is needful for Thy peace.

84. We Come As We Are

It is with a sense of enormous relief and reassurance, our Father, that we come into Thy presence with our lives as they are, confident that Thou dost understand us and deal with each of us in accordance with his needs. It is such a relief, our Father, not to be under any necessity to pretend anything to Thee but to be open and free, not trying to hide from Thy scrutiny but to spread before Thee the whole story, that which is good and that which is sordid, that which is worthy of the best in us, and that of which we are so terribly ashamed.

We make no demands upon Thy spirit; we ask nothing; we are in Thy presence as we are. O Love of God, love of God, do with us in this waiting moment what Thou wouldst do with us. We trust Thee, our Father, as best we can, and beyond that we yield to Thy grace, O God, our Father.

85. Our Sins We Remember

In Thy presence, our Father, our words seem so vain, so futile. Stand with us behind all of the pretensions of our lives, the prides, the boastings, the arrogances—all of the ways by which we seek to make secure the place for ourselves. Make tender our hearts, that we may be aware of all the ways by which Thou wouldst speak to us. Forgive us for our sins; they loom so large in the quietness. Our sins, we remember them. Lead us not into temptation, but deliver us from evil. This we would remember as we still ourselves in Thy presence, waiting for Thy benediction.

86. *The Burden of Pretensions*

Strong Son of God, immortal Love,
  Whom we, that have not seen Thy face,
  By faith, and faith alone, embrace,
Believing where we cannot prove;

. . . .

Our little systems have their day:
  They have their day and cease to be;
  They are but broken lights of Thee,
And Thou, O Lord, art more than they.

Close present Father, it is comforting and frightening to expose
our feelings, our impulses, our desires, and our thoughts to Thy
scrutiny. At last, to be utterly ourselves. What a relief to lift the
burden of pretensions. Weakness and strength, joy and sorrow,
sickness and health, pride and humility, hate and love shimmer
in the light of Thy countenance.

Forgive us for deliberate sin in which sometimes we take a
sneaky pride, in which at other times our shame breaks the heart
and our tears flow without hindrance. Forgive us for the moments
when in perverse self-defense our hearts have hardened, and with
our own hands we have closed the doors of our spirits against the
agony of our fellows.

O God, without whom life is void of all meaning and in whom
there is all that is, share the tenderness of Thy strength so per-
vasively within us that no one will be turned empty from our
door and no voice that cries for help will go unheeded. Teach us
how to respond to the needs of Thy children in ways that do not
undermine the self, but inspire and enliven the spirit! And perhaps,
just perhaps, it is not too much to hope that in us Thou wilt
rejoice and take delight!

87. The Logic of Our Past

Our Father, we come again to Thee, searching our minds for some fresh way to give expression to the common needs and particular urgencies of our private lives. We are comforted that Thou art not overmuch concerned with the words we use. We rest in the assurance that Thou searchest out the hidden things of the heart, the central concerns of our living, the hopes, the fears, the yearnings that inform the quality of our deeds. There is something within us that wants to be good, to be kind, to be gentle, while there is so much that is stubborn and unyielding. In so many ways we are fettered by the logic of our past—we would be free, but under Thy scrutiny we are aware that we are our own jailer.

Purge us of all that obscures our vision and keeps us from the living sense of Thy living Presence. All of this is a desperate way to say that we want the strength to do Thy will and the honesty to seek that strength. Wilt Thou accept this and do with it in us what Thy great heart desires? We give to Thee simple thanks from simple hearts.

88. *Let Us Be Transparent*

Deliver us from the tempests of our inward churnings. Calm our spirits with Thy great tranquillities, that we may be total instruments in Thy hands, to serve Thy purposes and share in Thy work in the world. Let us be transparent, that Thy Light may not be dimmed in us and through us no darkness may come to those whose trust we have and whose hands are in our hands.

These are the words; behind them are the urgencies of the heart. Let the words and the urgencies be a living sacrament placed upon Thy altar even as did our Master.

89. Our Brittle Lives

O Lord, make clean our hearts within us. We have no new words by which to lay before Thee the story of our brittle lives and our present needs, the thirst of our hearts, the sorrow, pain, and tragedy of certain of our experiences, the joys and the illuminations by which our steps are made secure. We are as little children walking along the seashore, admiring here and there a pebble for its beauty and its shape, while all that we would be, would sense, would feel and would understand stretches out before us, boundless and unexplored. Be patient with us, O Lord, be patient, that we may learn how to walk in the light which has been made so luminous by many who have gone before us in our journey.

90. A Great Rejoicing!

Close present Father, we come seeking no gifts, no offering, making no requests of Thee. How good it is to feel this way and how strange! All that we feel today is a great rejoicing, that we are privileged to spread our lives before Thee, presuming to make no demands upon Thy love. It is enough to be ourselves utterly before Thee . . . and to wait for the movement of Thy spirit within us.

V

Postscriptions

We have tried, our Father, to make articulate the stirring of the mind and heart that is just out of reach. We make as an offering to Thee even our failure. Walk beside us in our journeying and leave us not alone even to the devices of our minds and spirits, but be in us and about us, forever and ever.

The empty word,
the broken phrase,
the stumbling thought—
these we place upon
Thy altar, O God.
Sanctify them with Thy truth
even as Thou dost sanctify us with Thy truth.
Walk with us in the way that we take,
lest our footsteps stumble
in the darkness and we lose
our way, our Father.

With a deep sense of confidence we turn our thoughts and all of the overtones of our feelings in Thy direction, O God, our Father. Brood over us, cleansing and renewing and restoring, to the end that we may face the responsibilities that await us beyond this moment with strength, with confidence, and with courage.

Forgive us, our Father, for all the things of which we are so poignantly aware and for those failures of will that have made it so difficult for us to respond to Thy will. Walk with us in the long, perilous journey which stretches out before us and give to our faltering footsteps the great, strong rhythm of the purposes of God.

Forgive us, our Father,
for all the failures by which
we have responded
to Thy love and Thy truth.
Keep our spirits tender
and our minds and hearts
sensitive to Thyself,
that we may not spend our years
wandering in the darkness.

Walk with us as we wrestle to find a way to reveal Thy life and Thy spirit and Thy mind, O God, that we may be true to the light.

And therefore, for love's sake, then,
I will do what no power
in heaven or hell or on the earth
could make me do if I did not love.
So, God, as experience must be like this,
I would not snare Thee in a web of words,
I would not try to reduce
all the vast reaches of Thy meaning
to paltry symbols.
I would but open myself to Thee
and let Thy spirit invade me
and fill me until I do not know
what is mine or Thine.
This would be my fulfillment,
O my God!